Fairy Mandala

Stress Relieving Adult Coloring Book

Copyright: Published in the United States by Bee Book.
Published July 2019

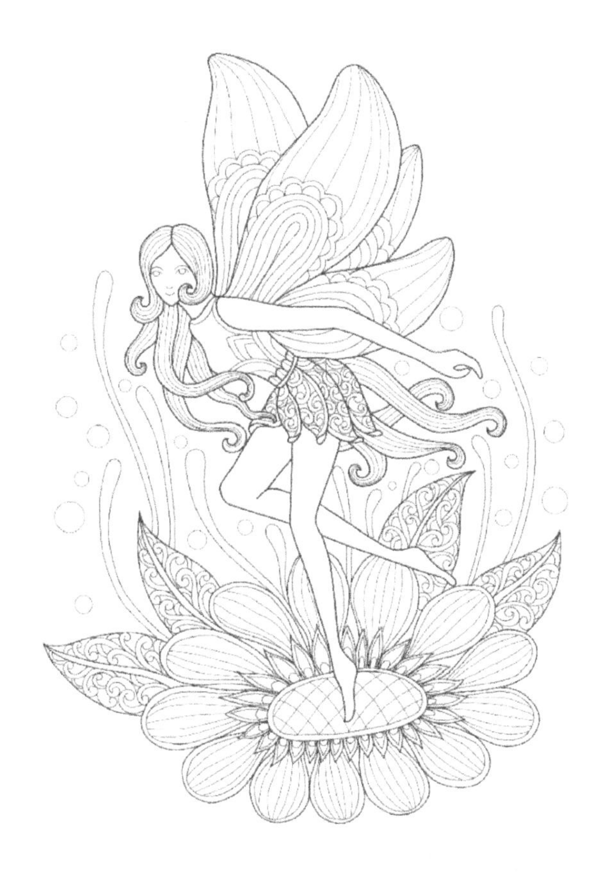

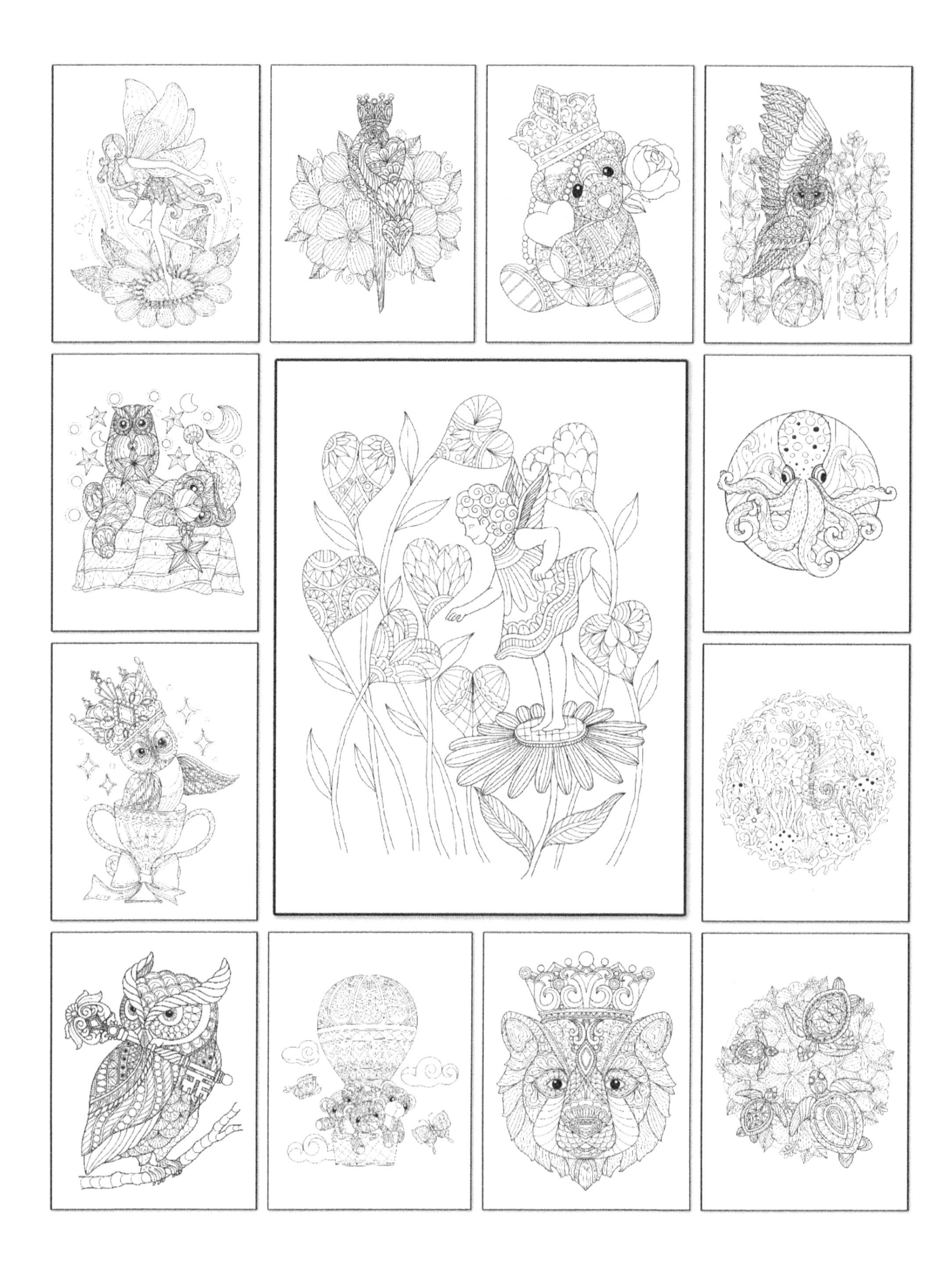

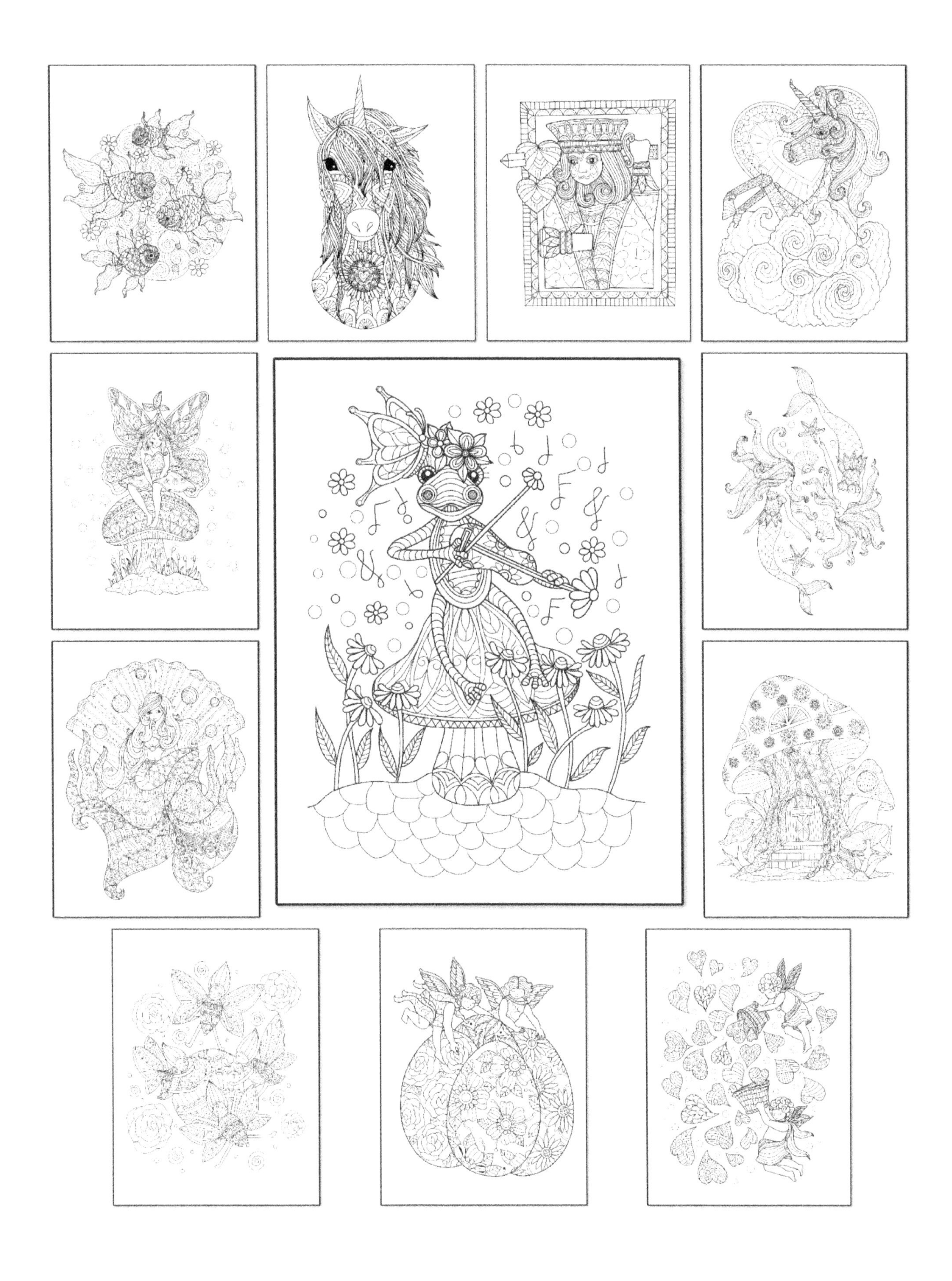

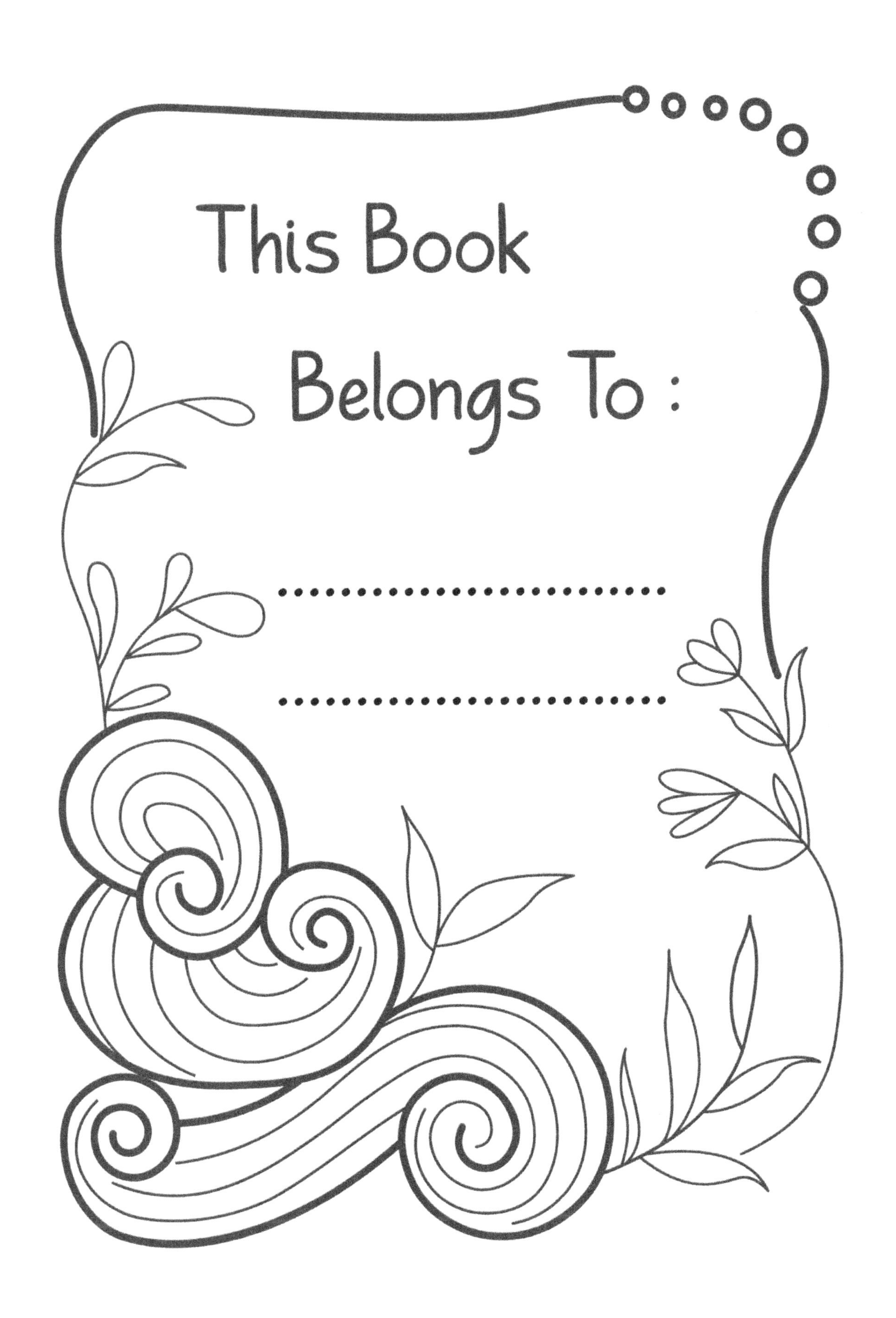
This Book
Belongs To :
....
....

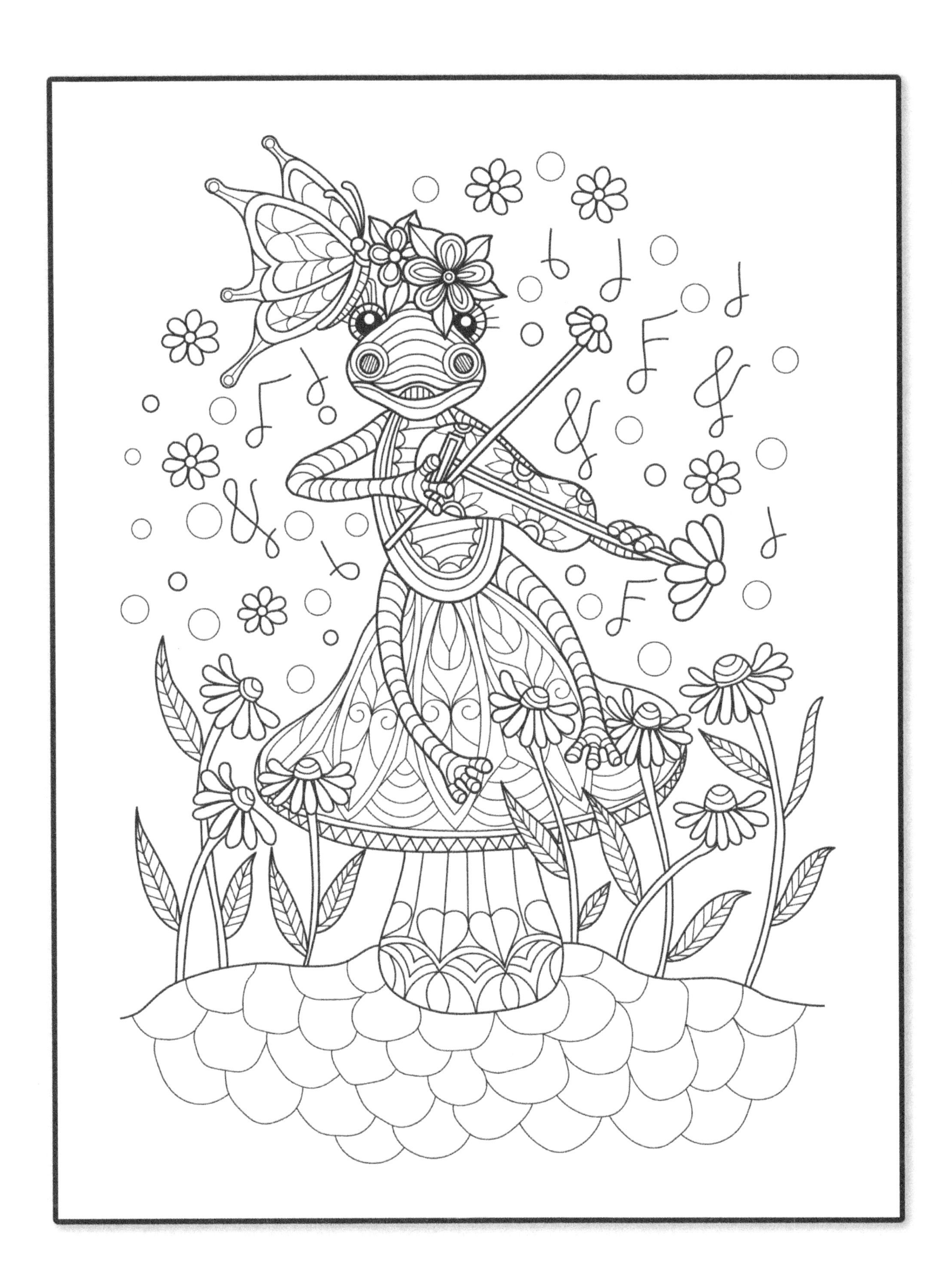

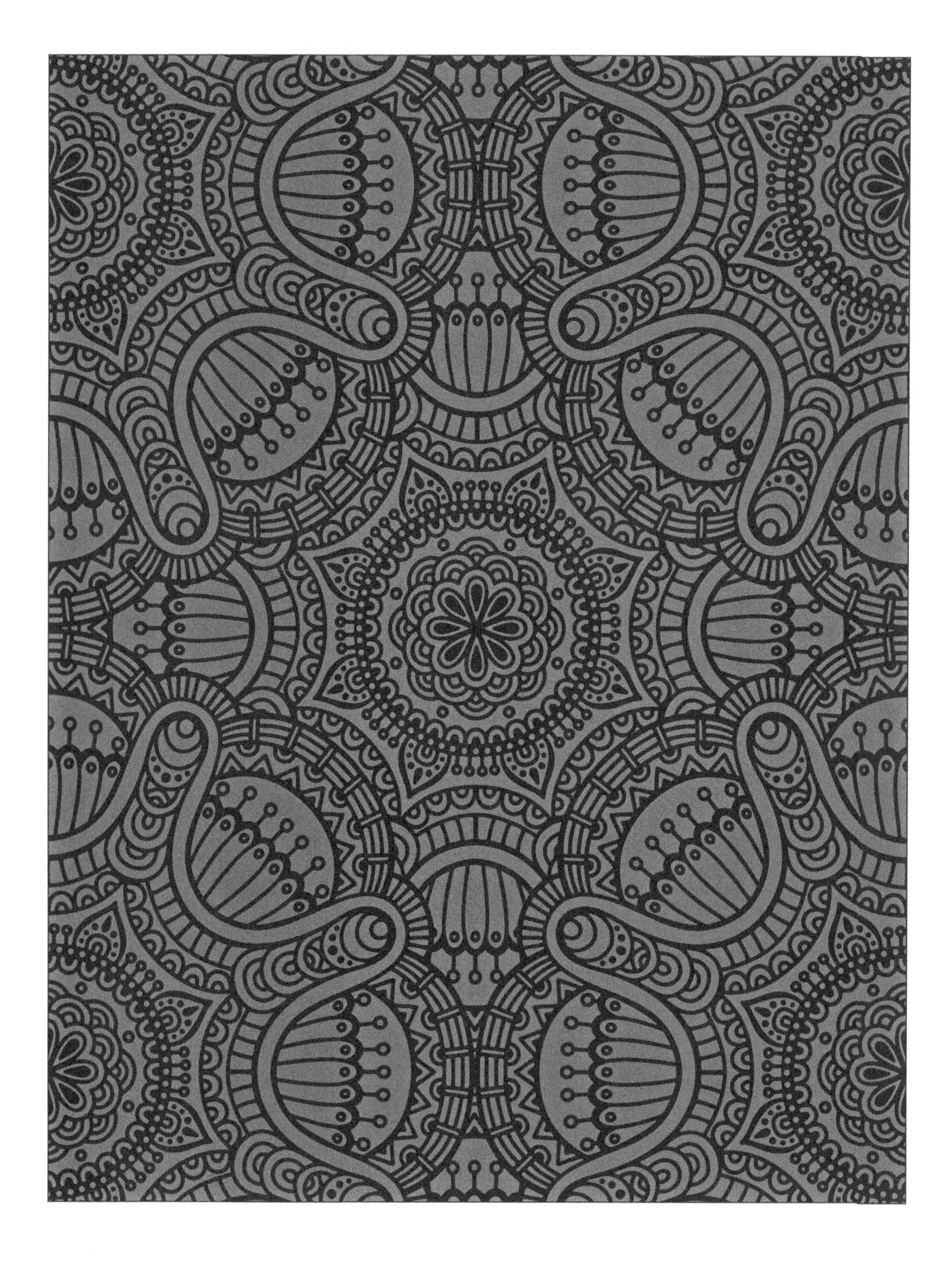

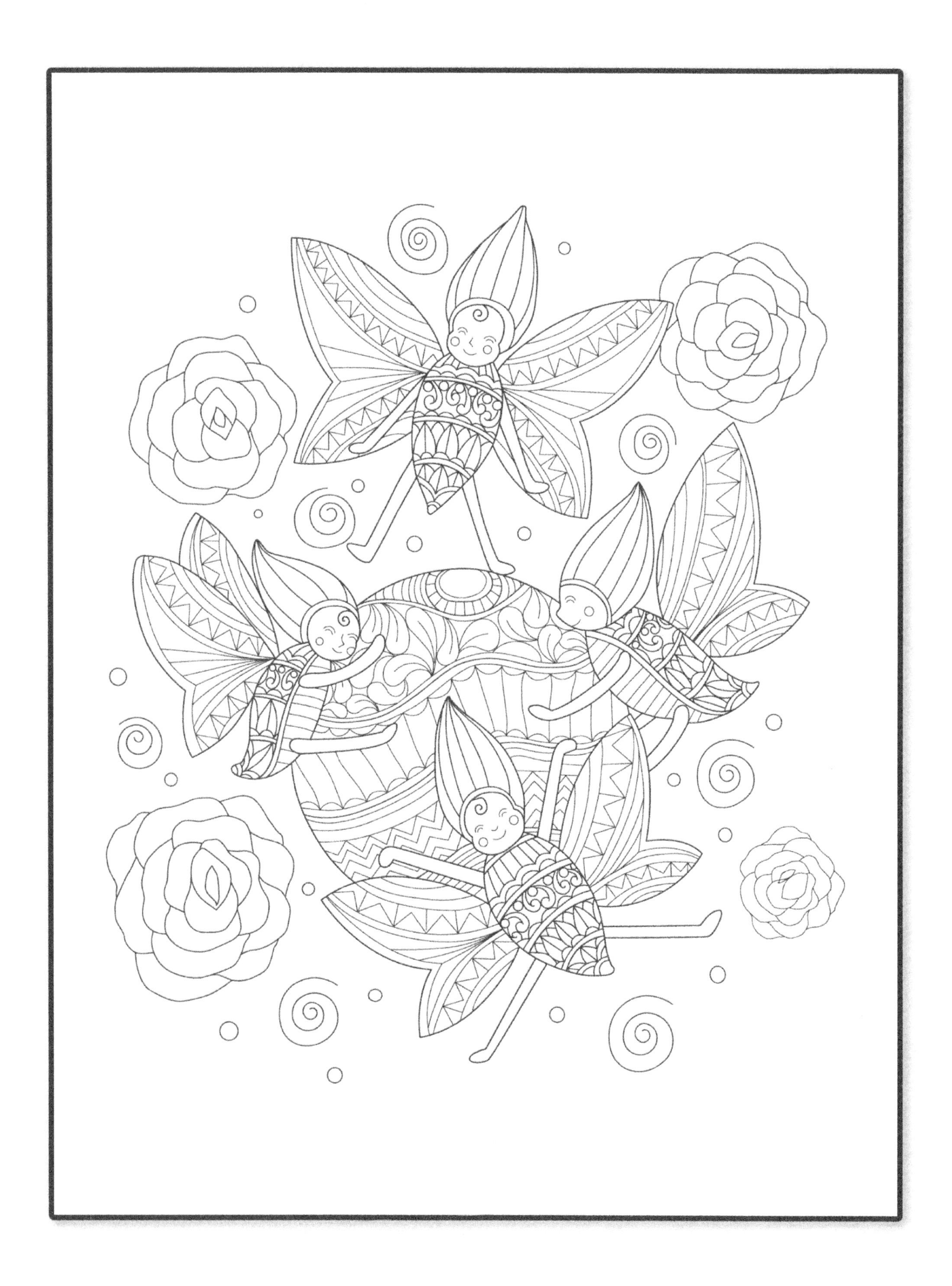

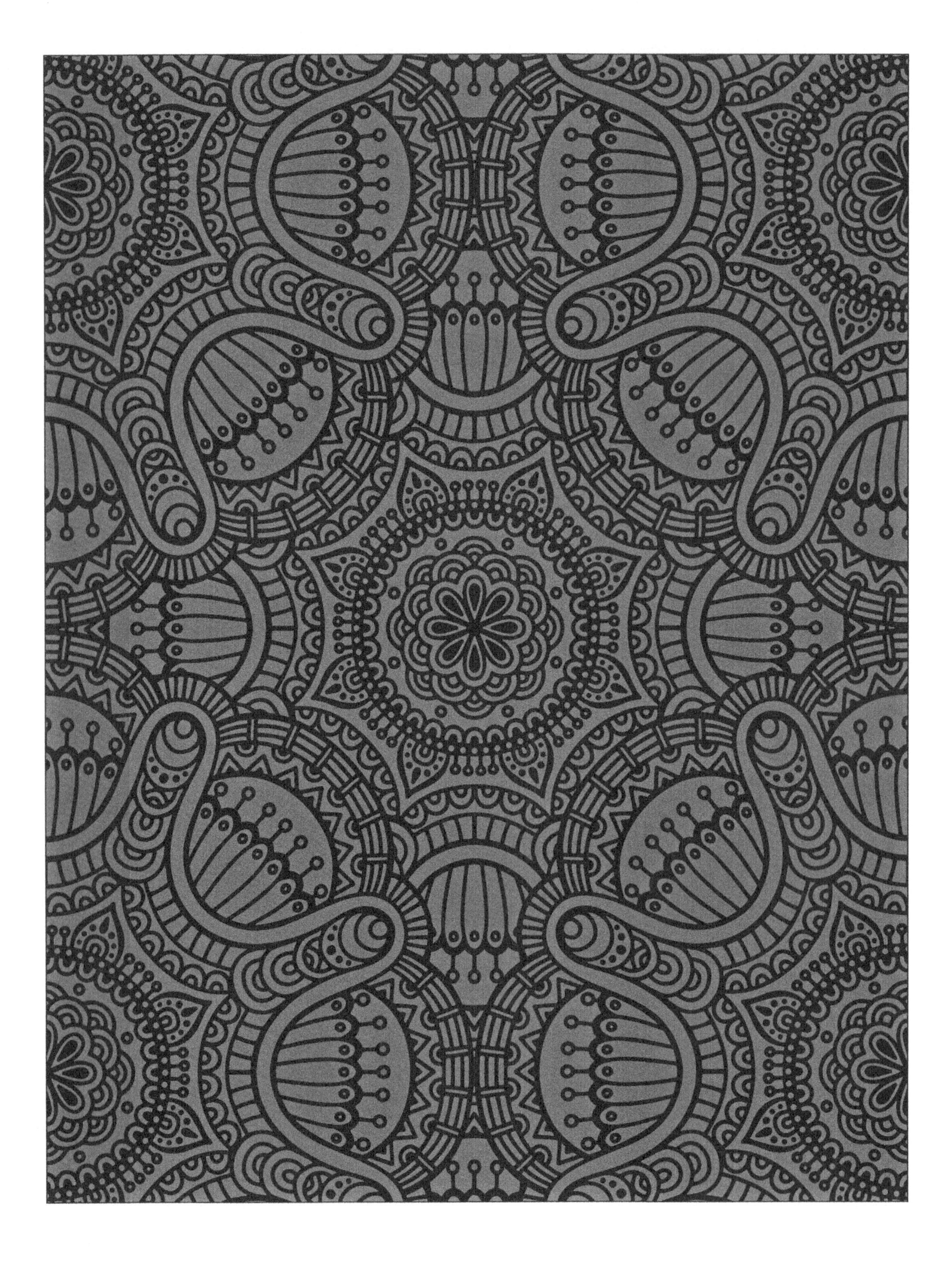

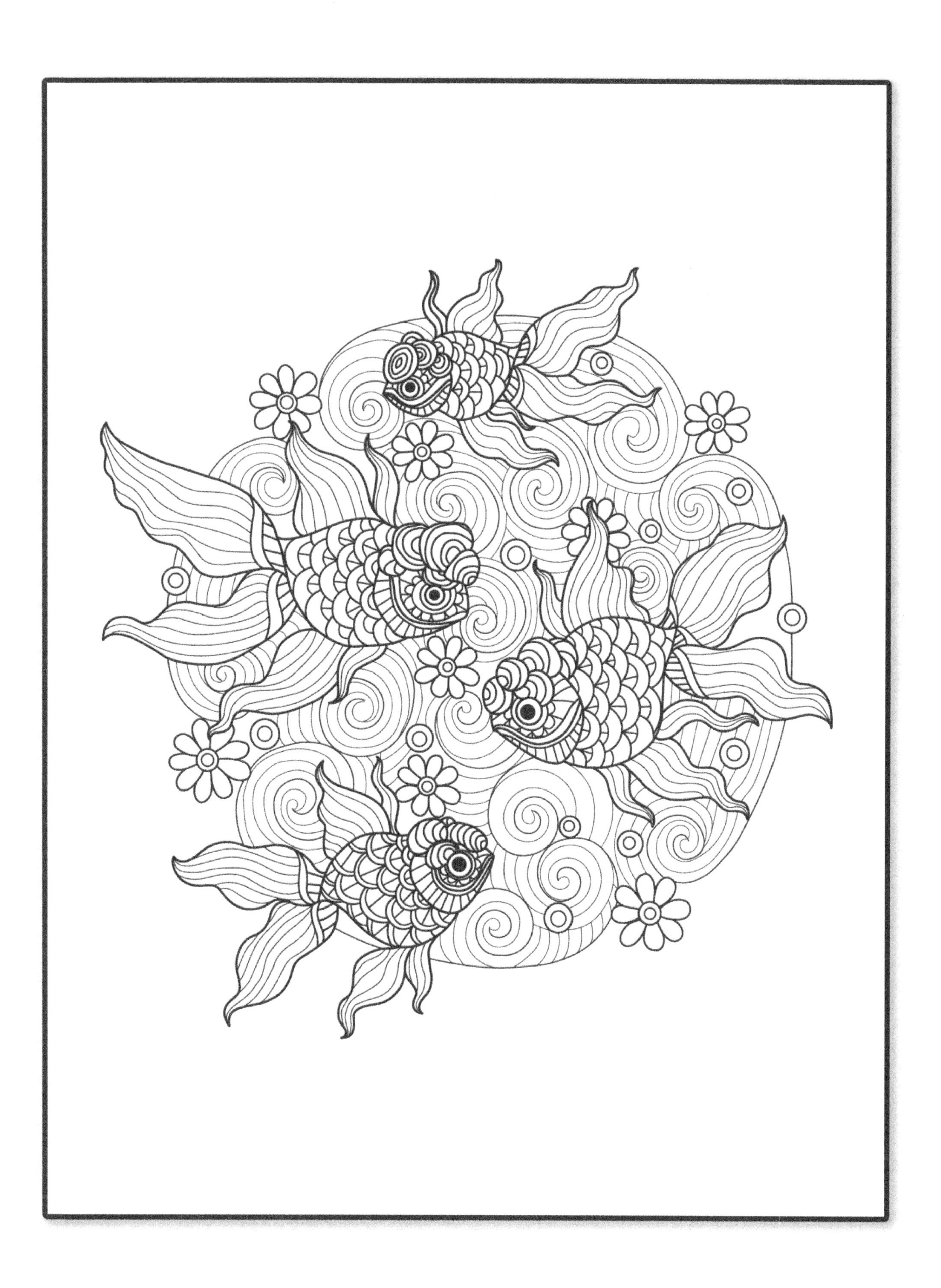

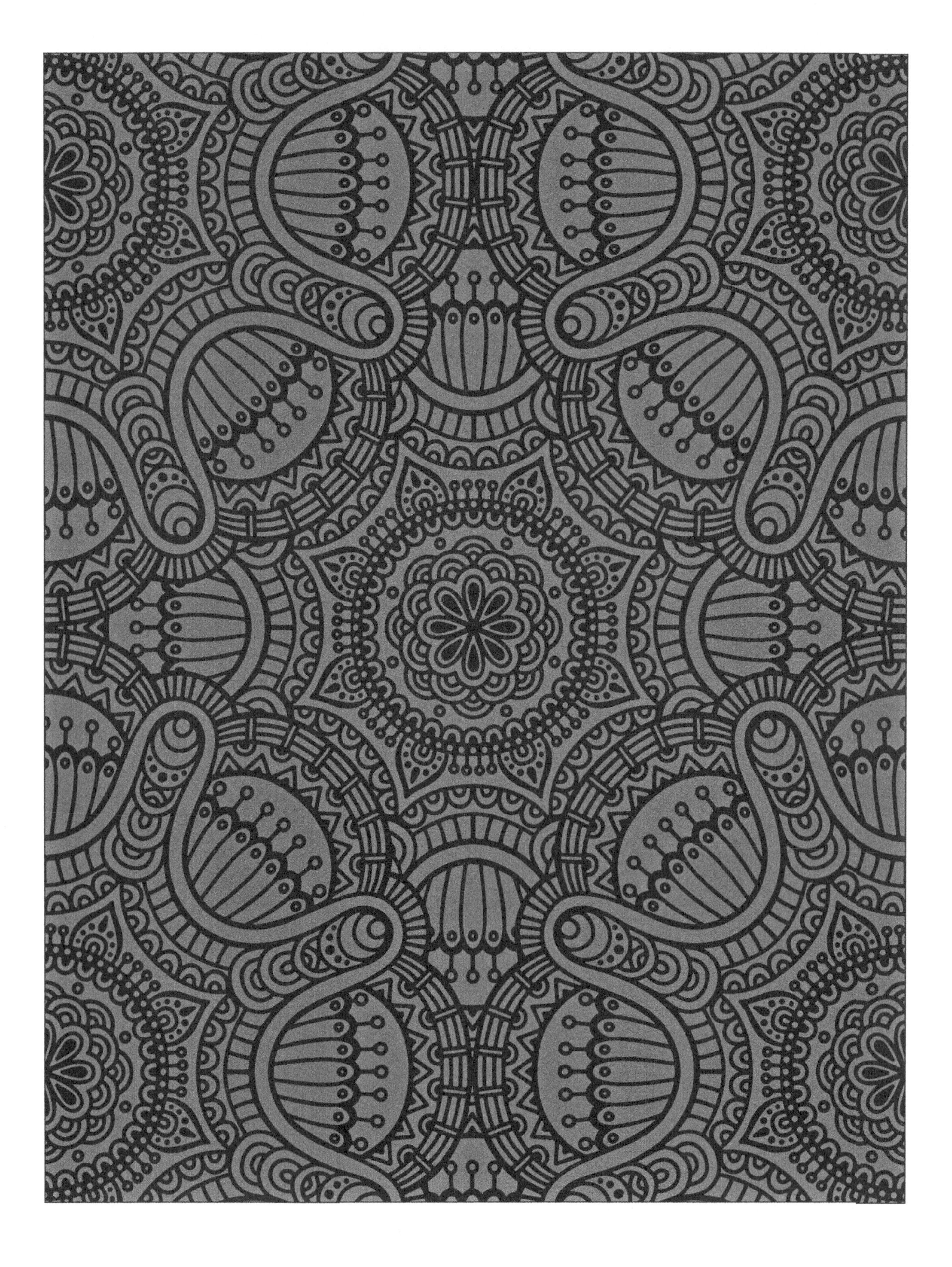

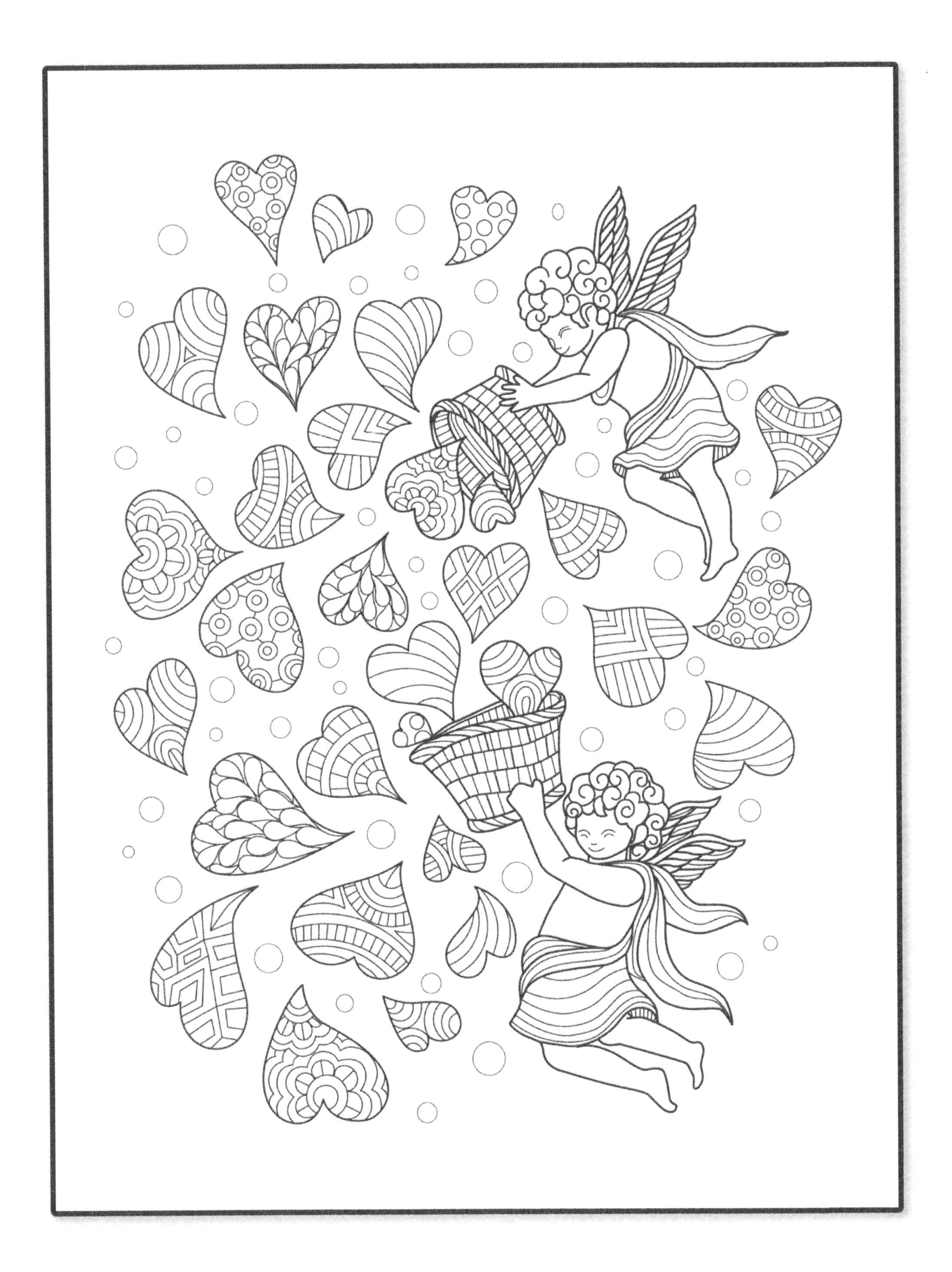

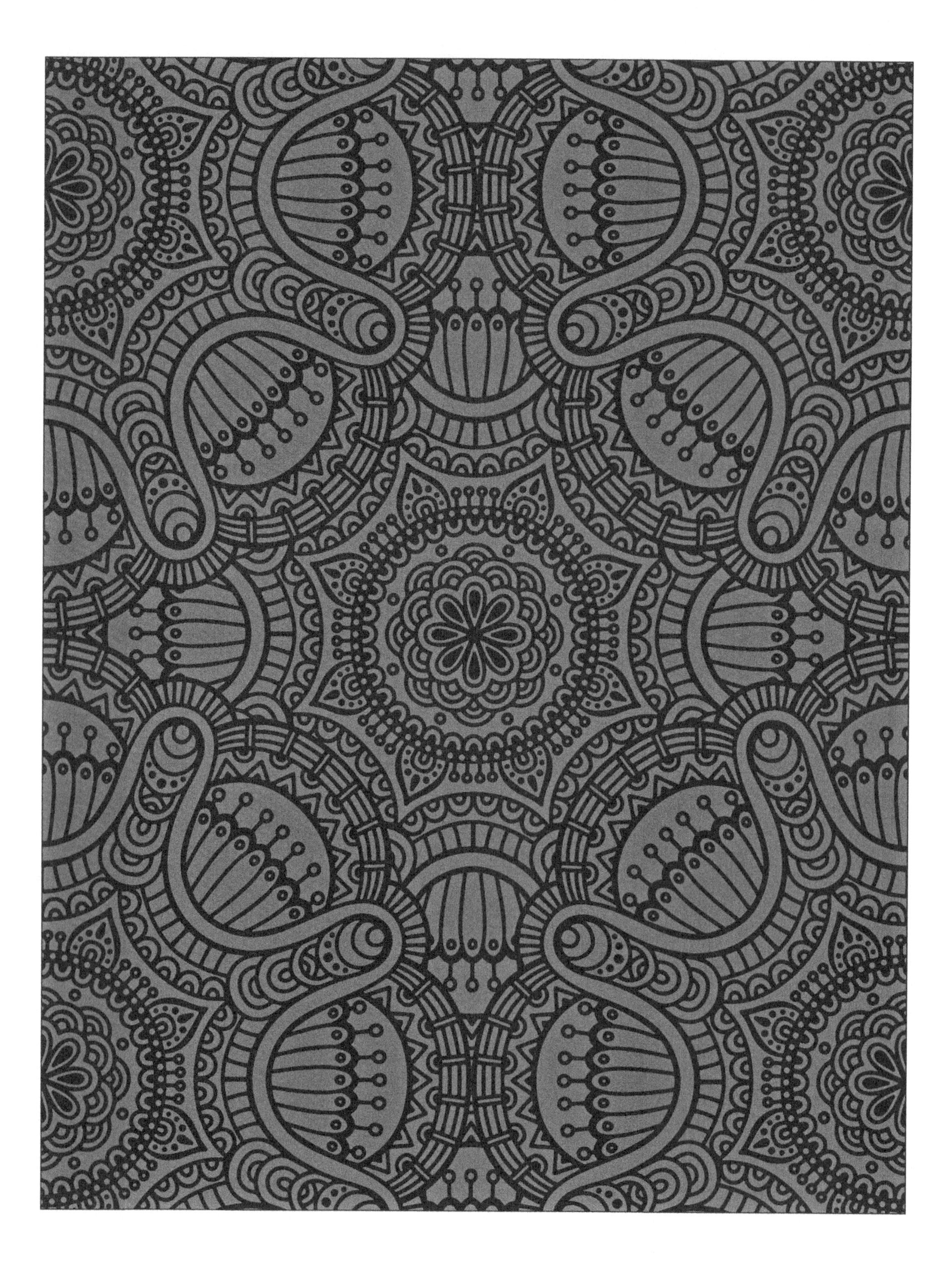

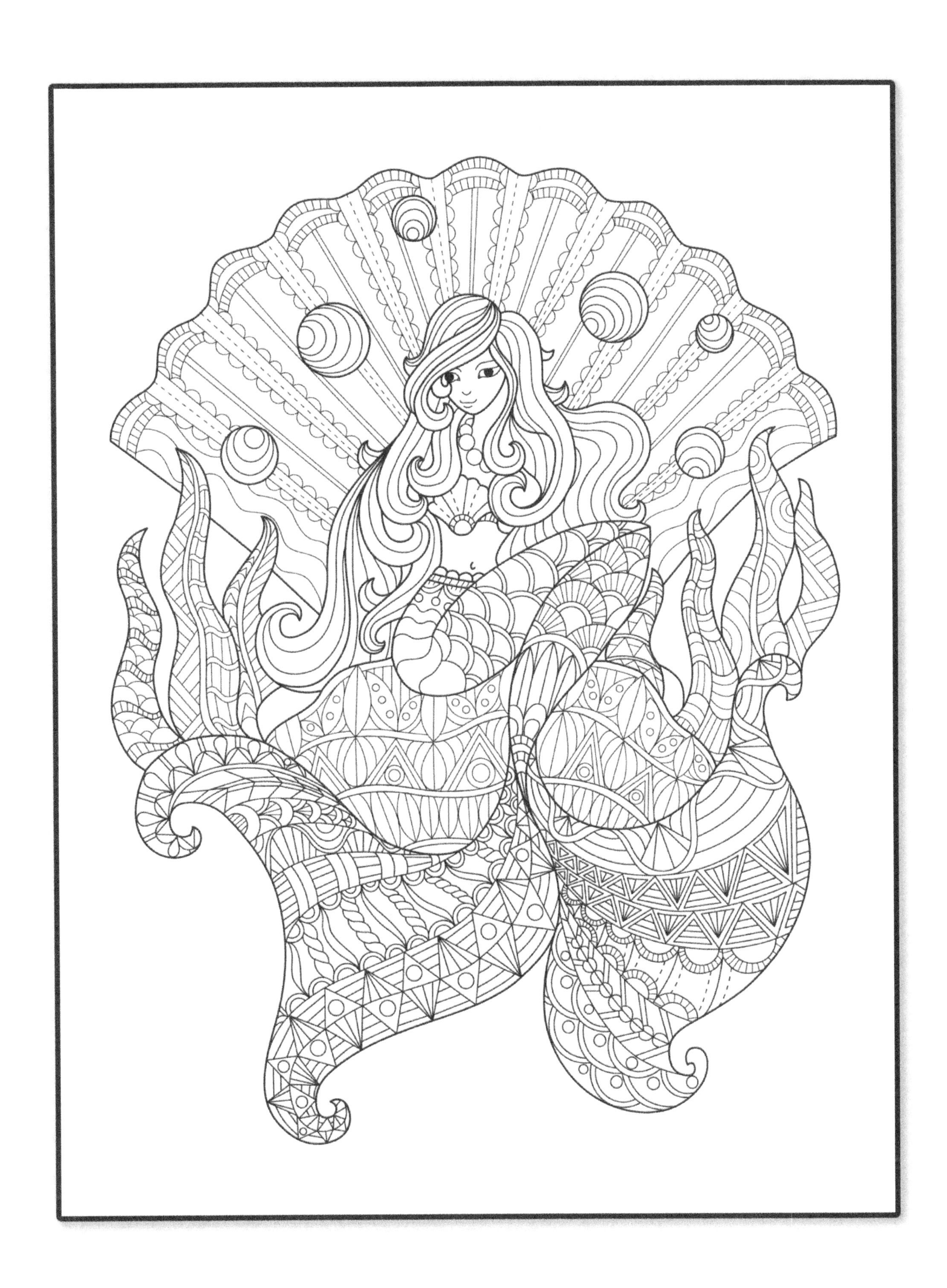

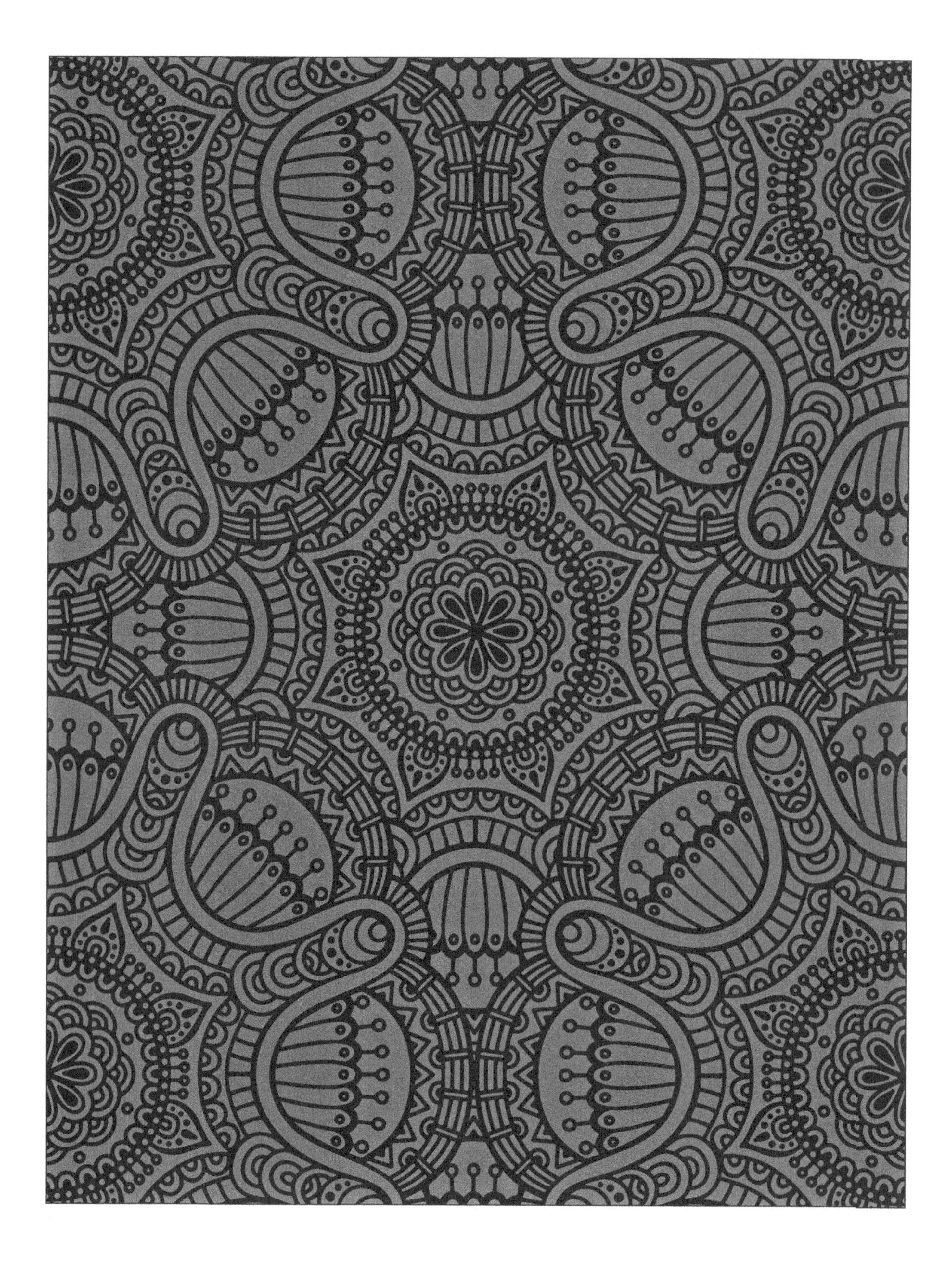

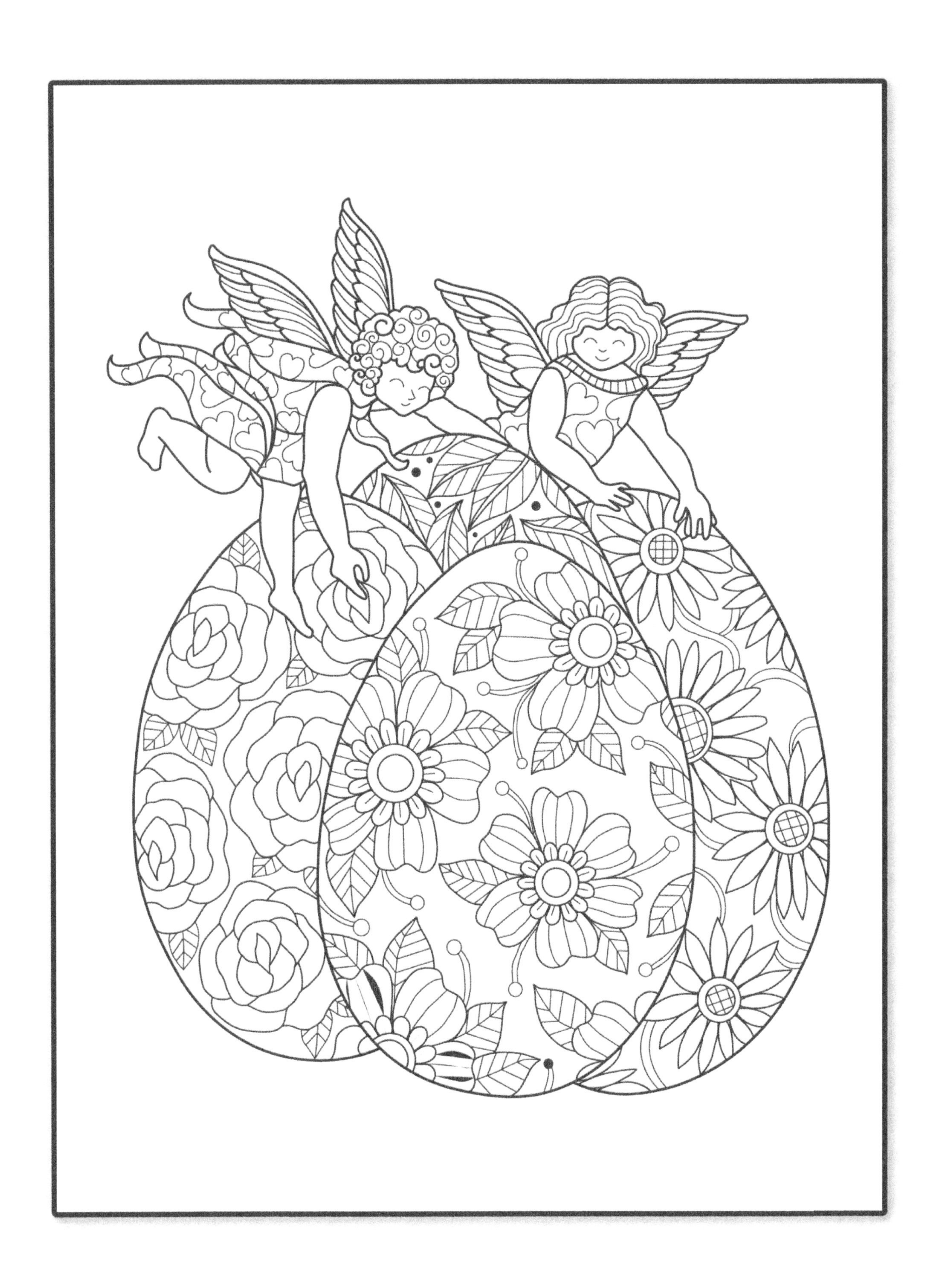

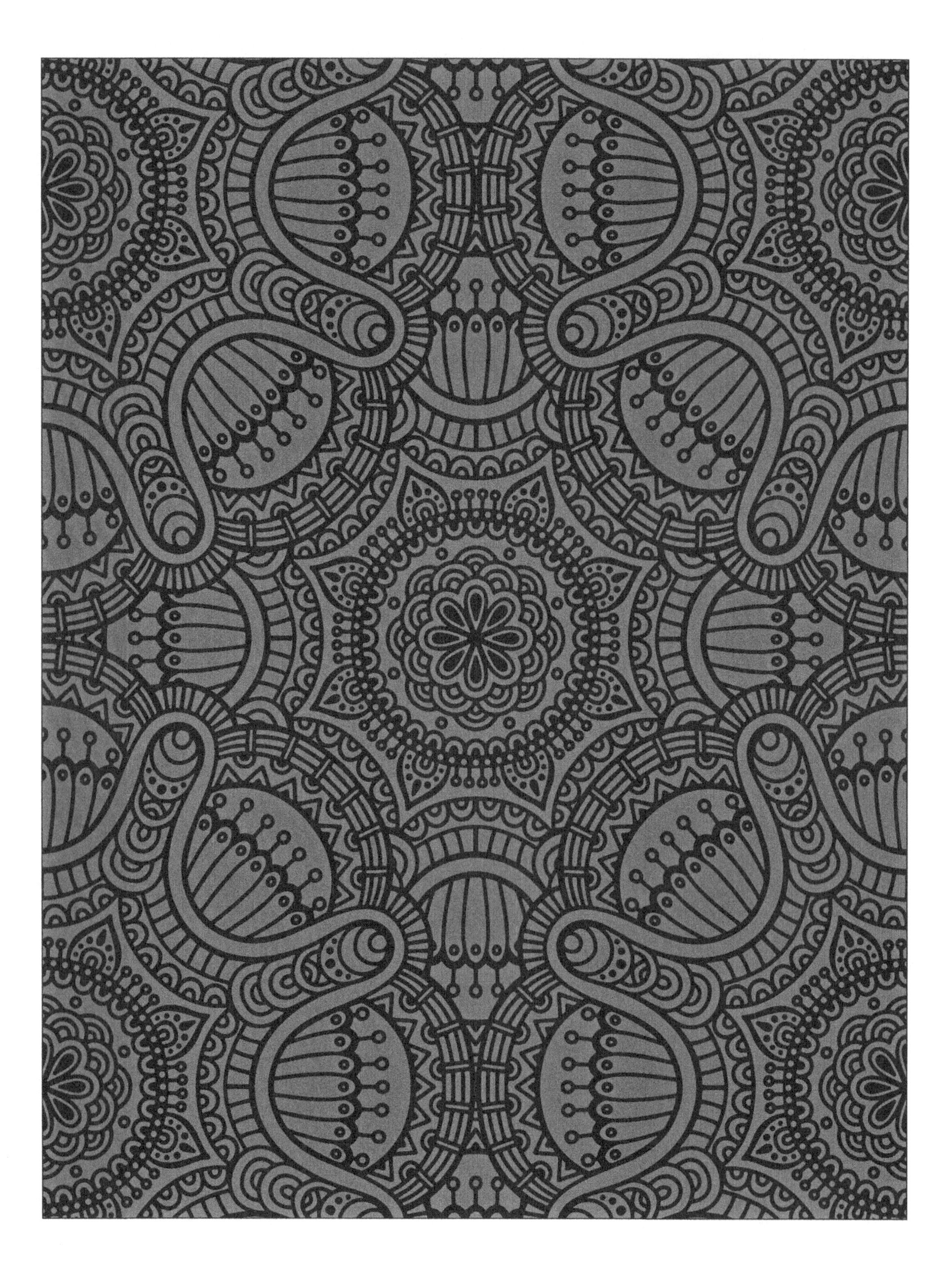

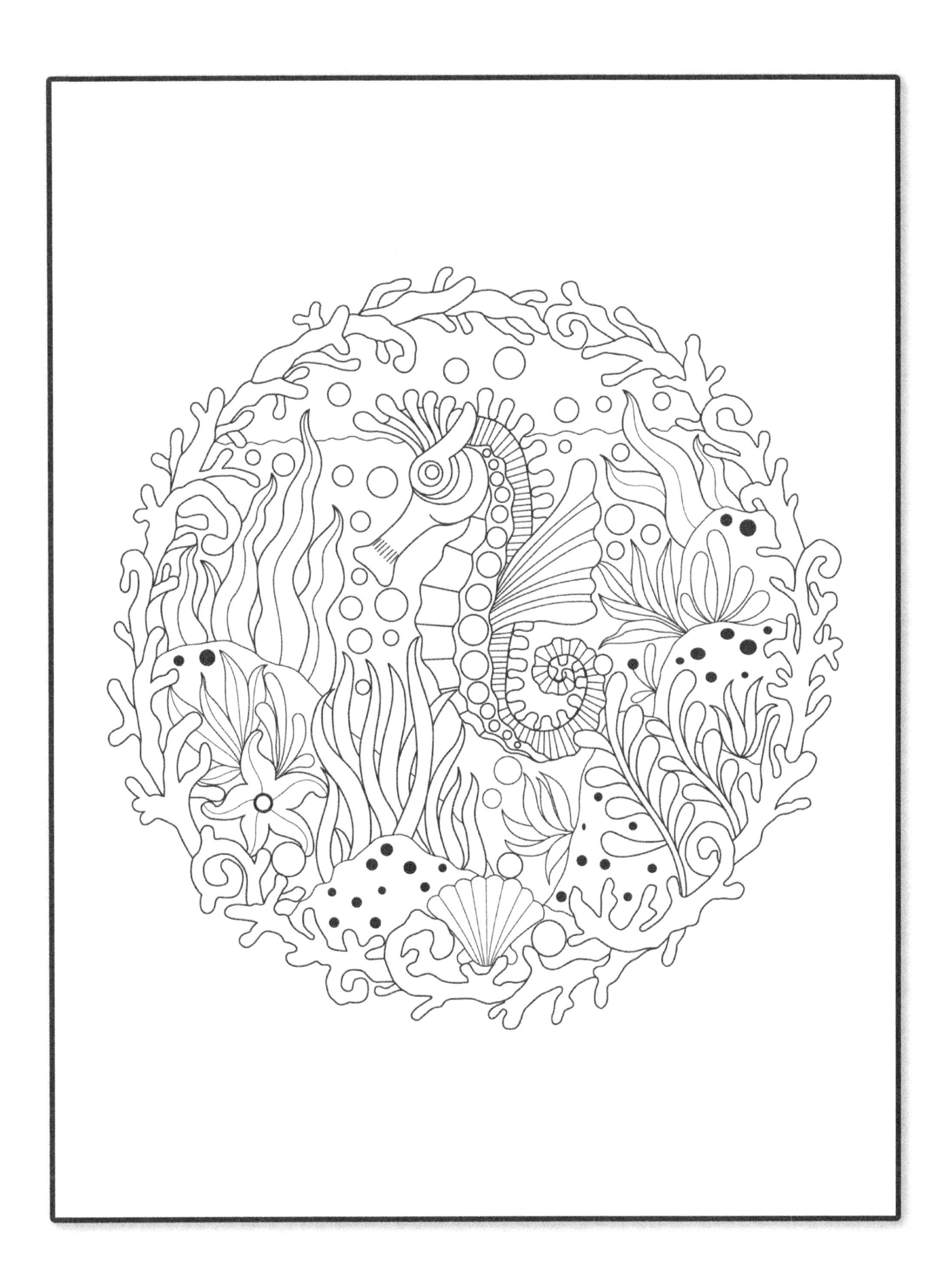

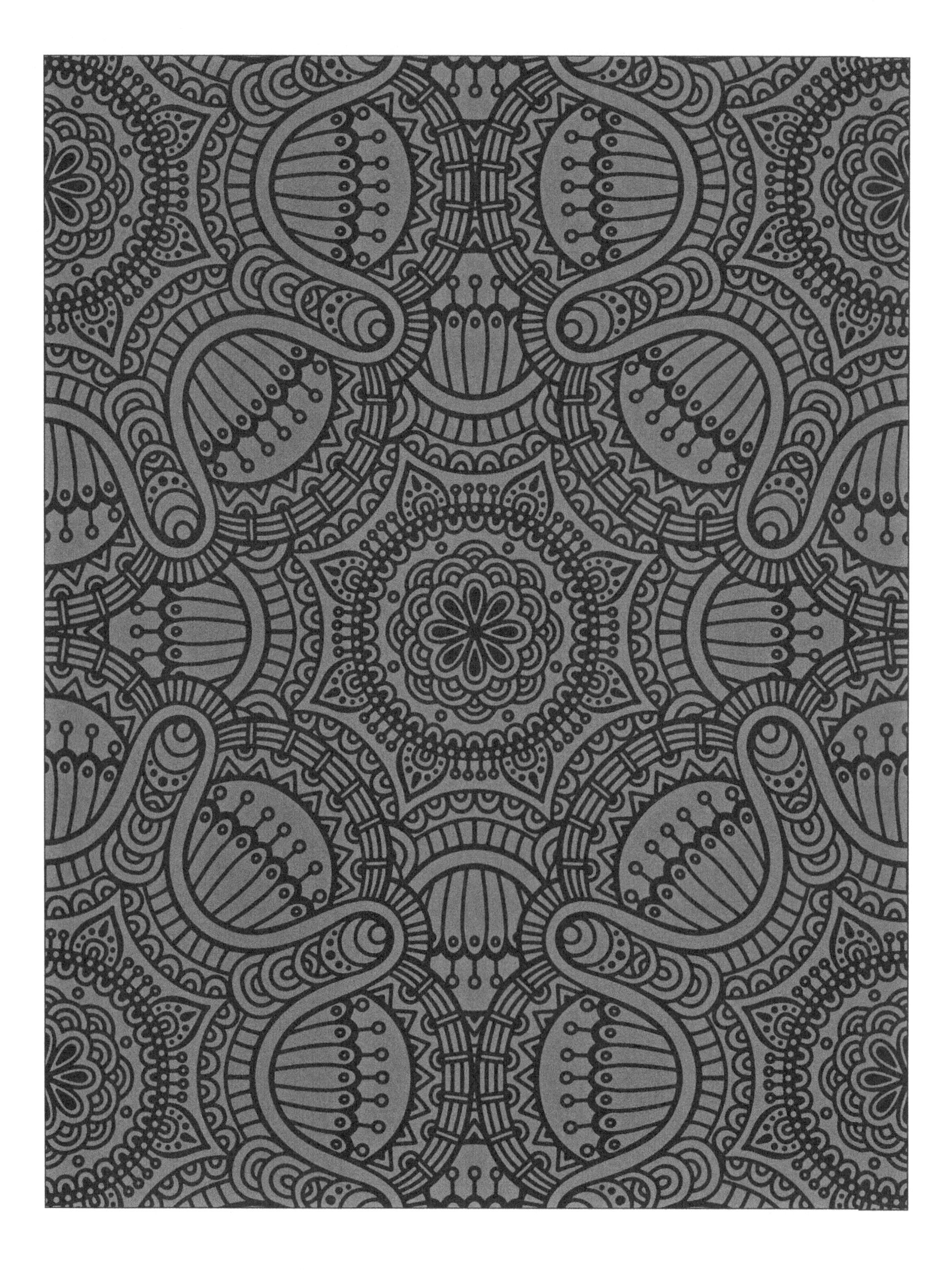

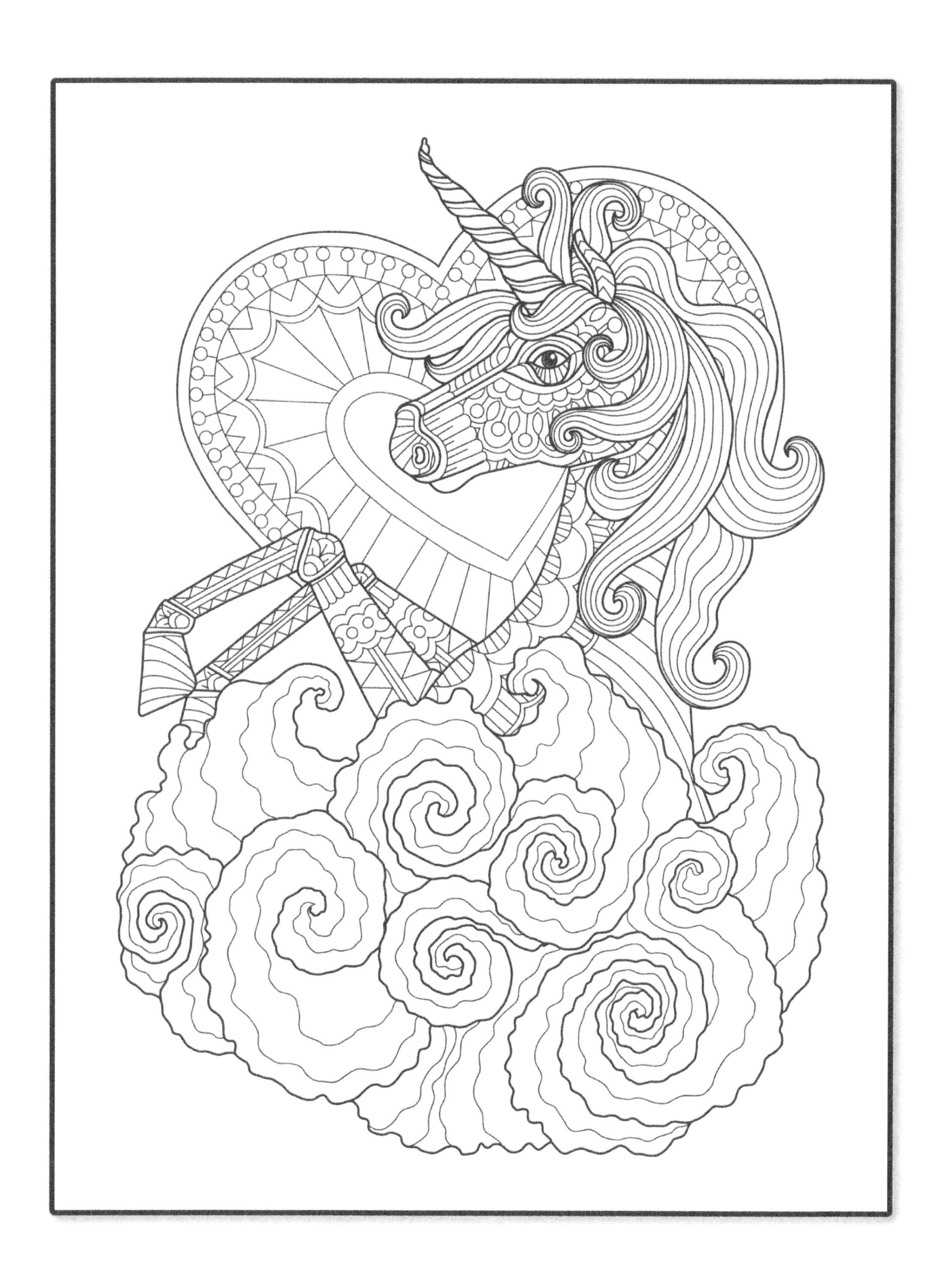

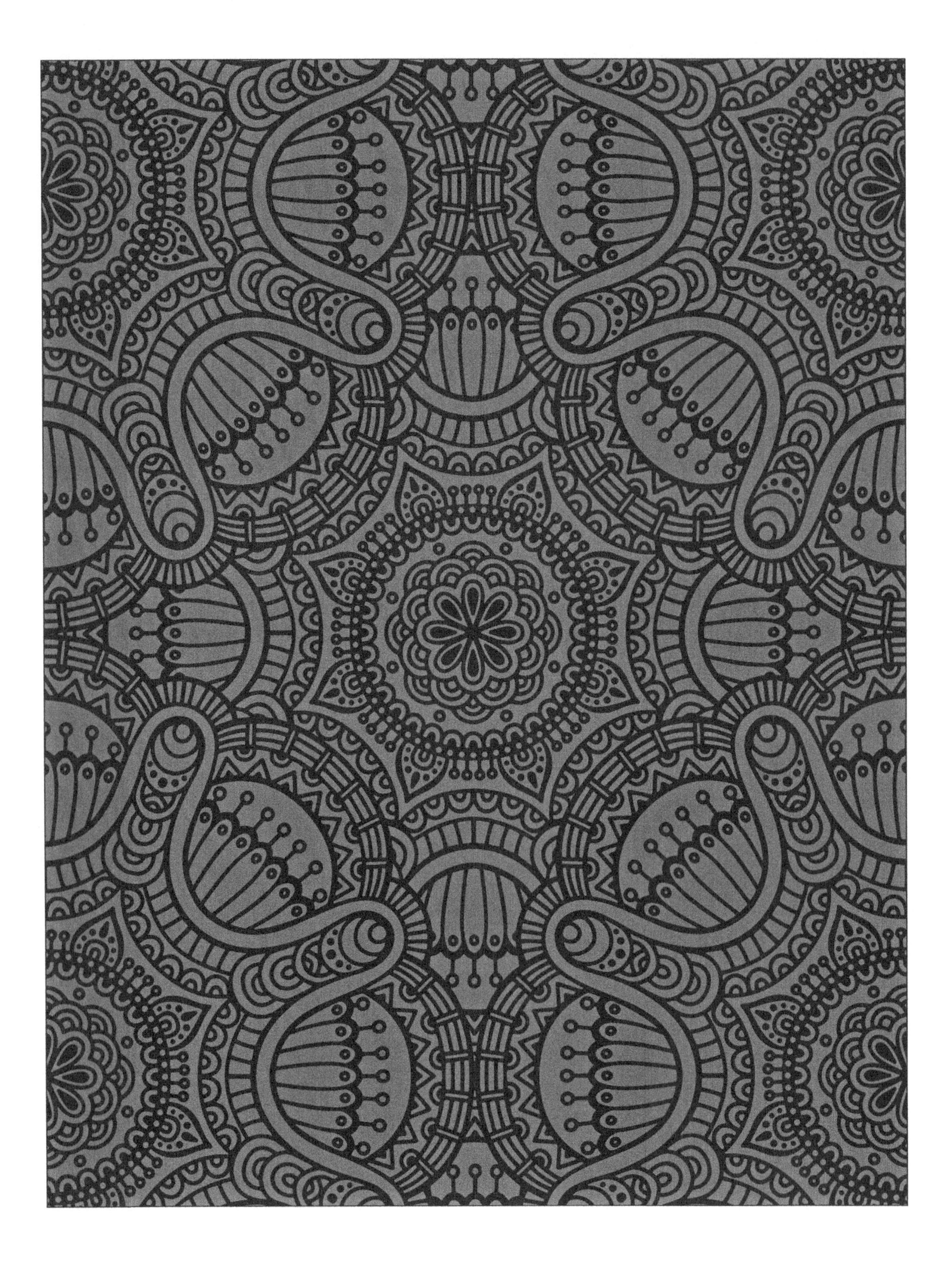

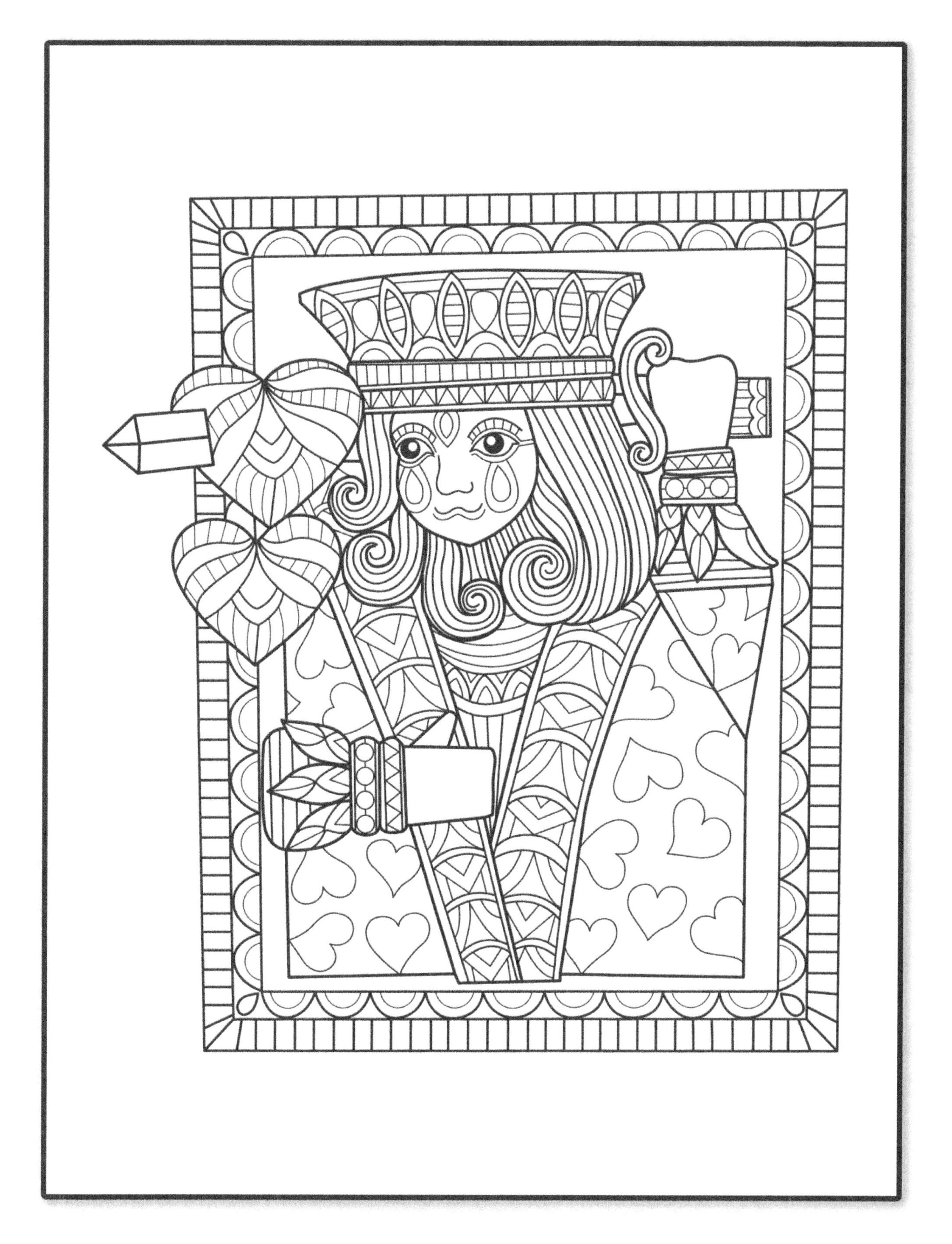

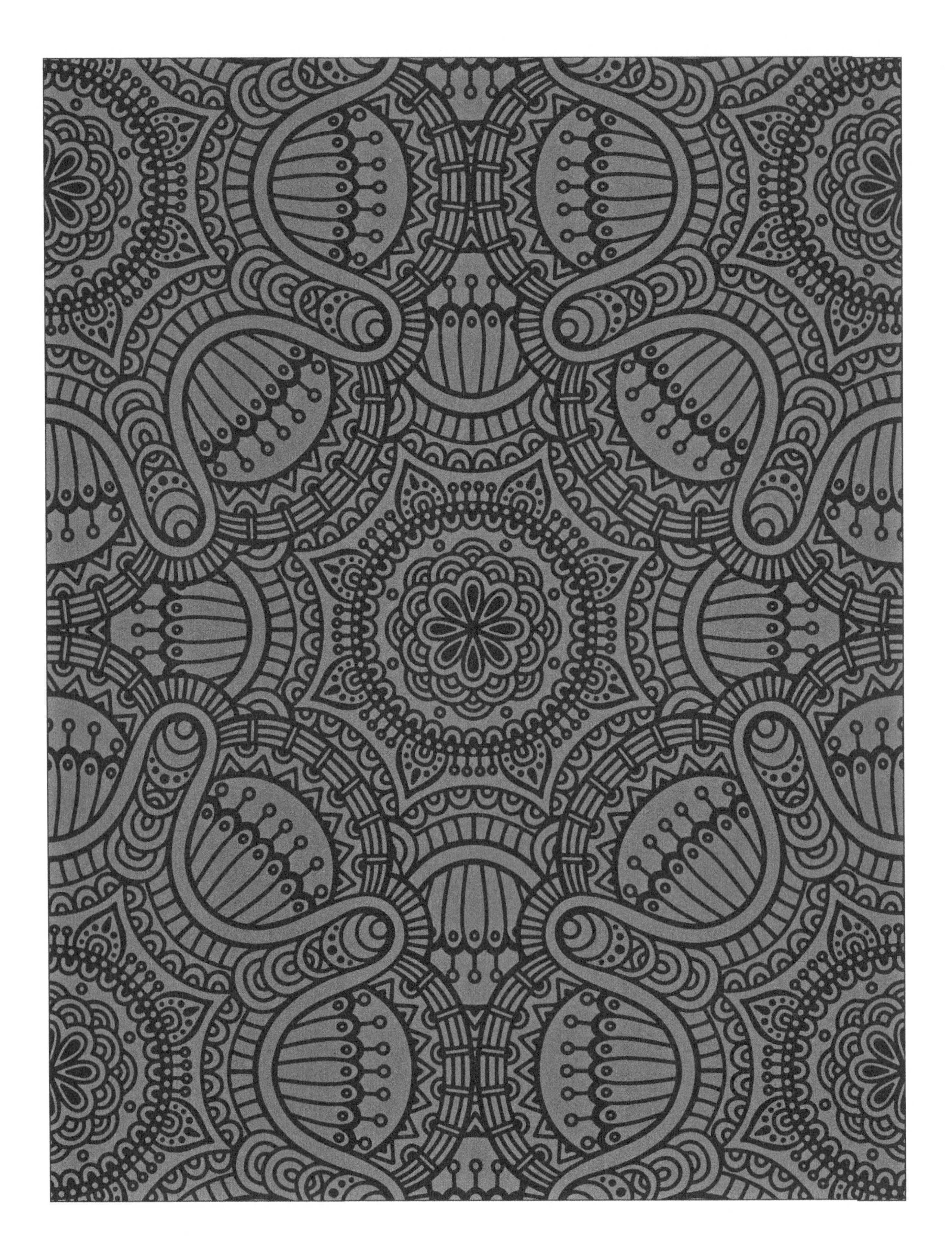

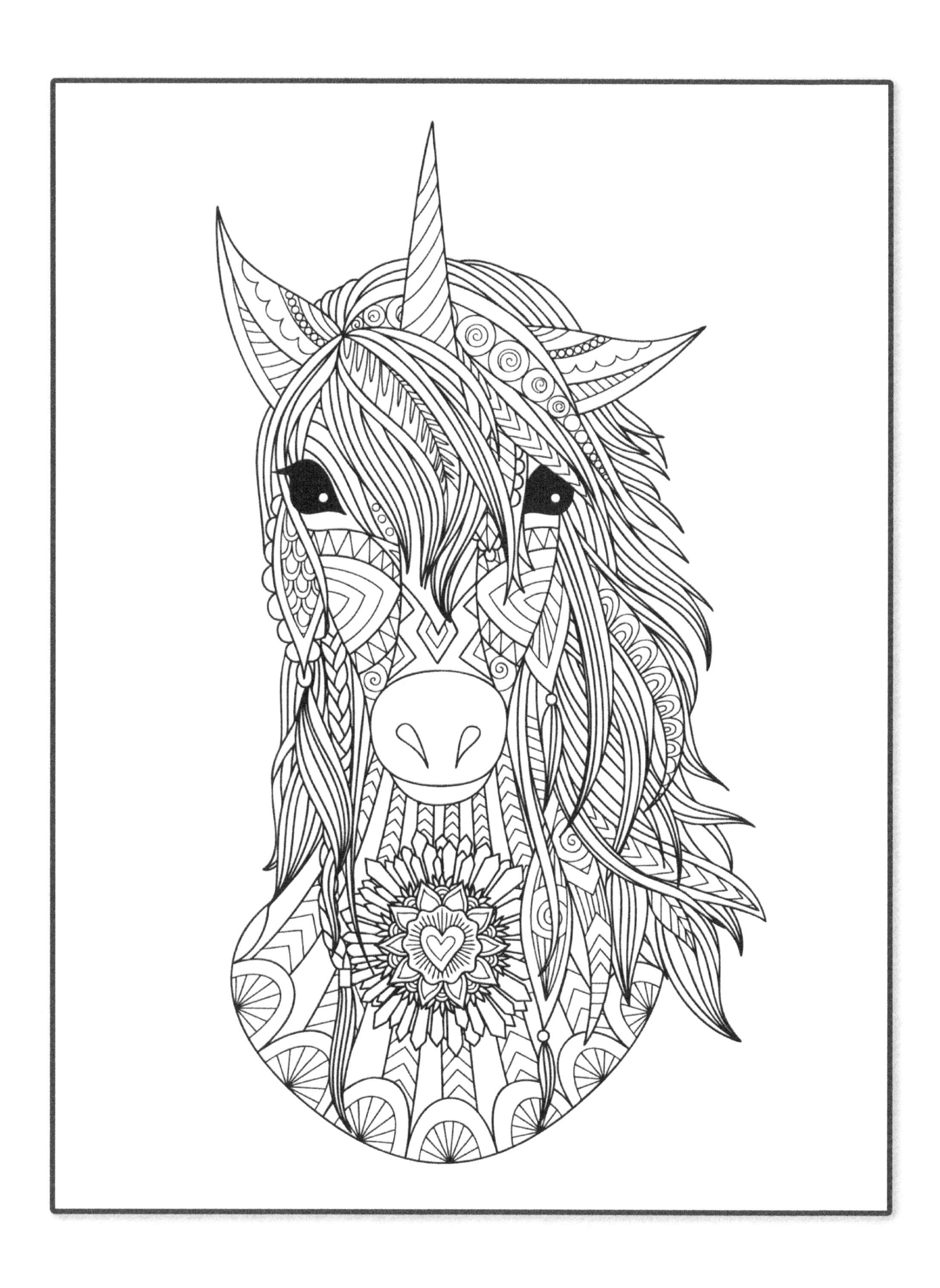

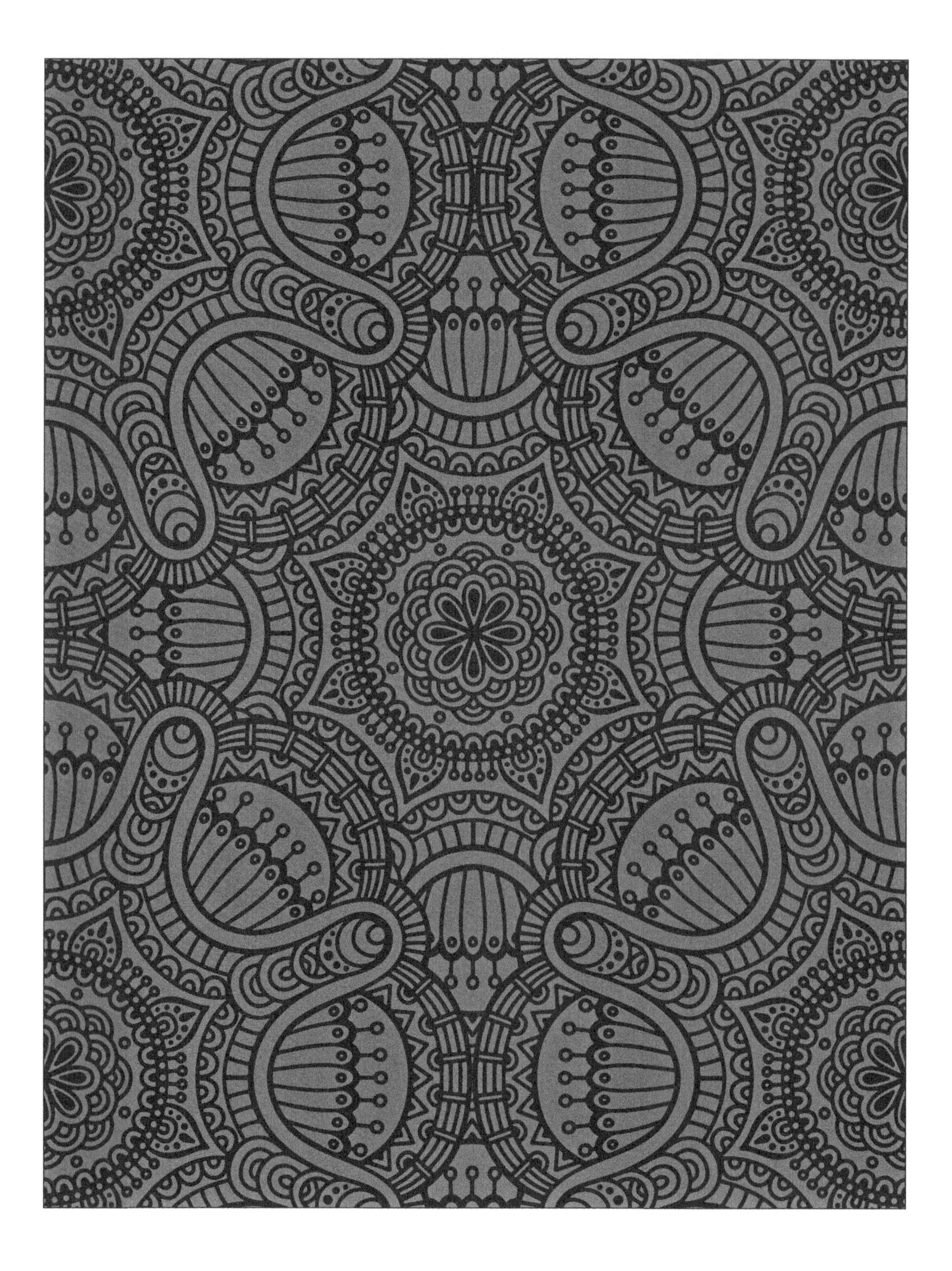

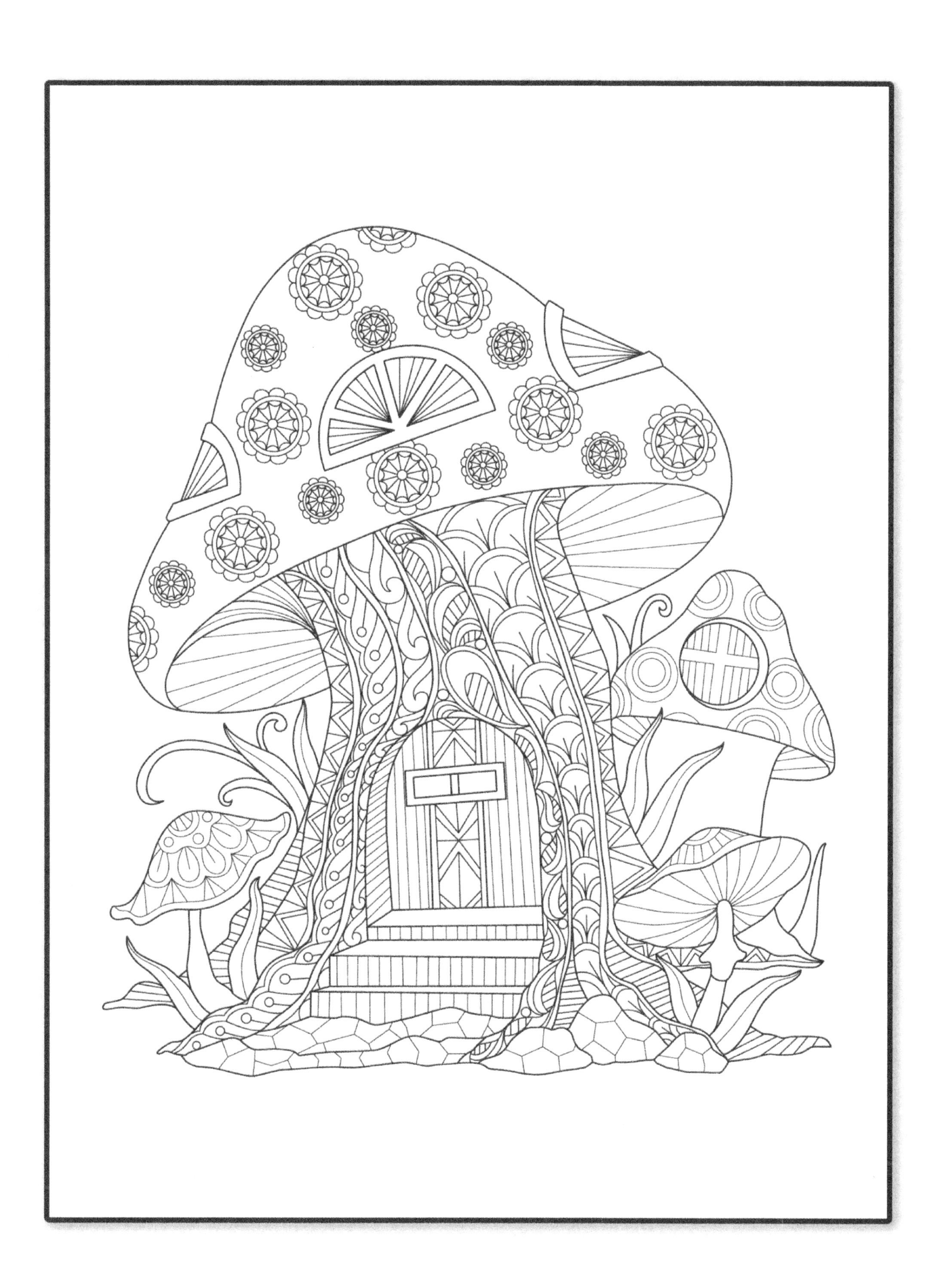

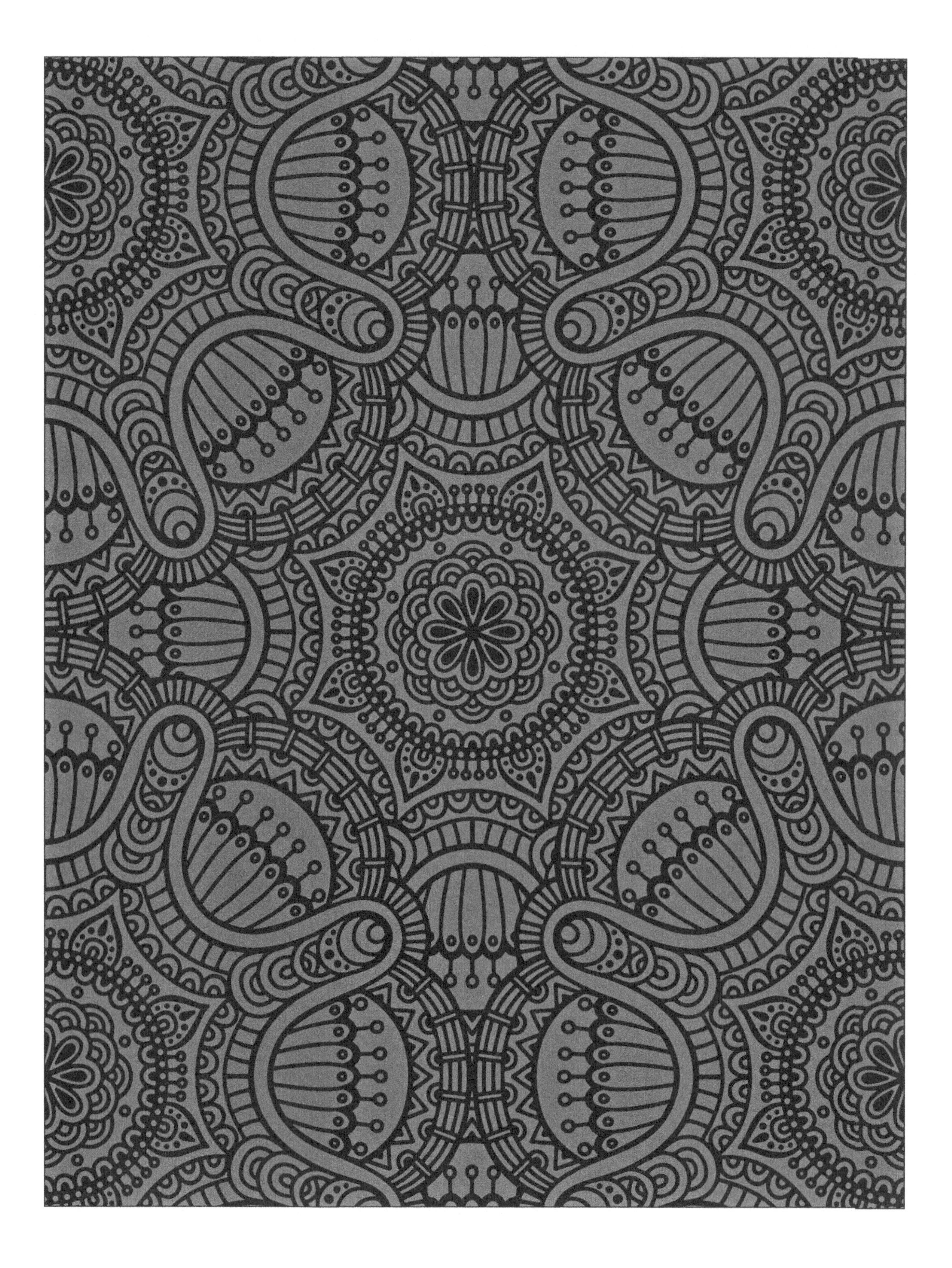

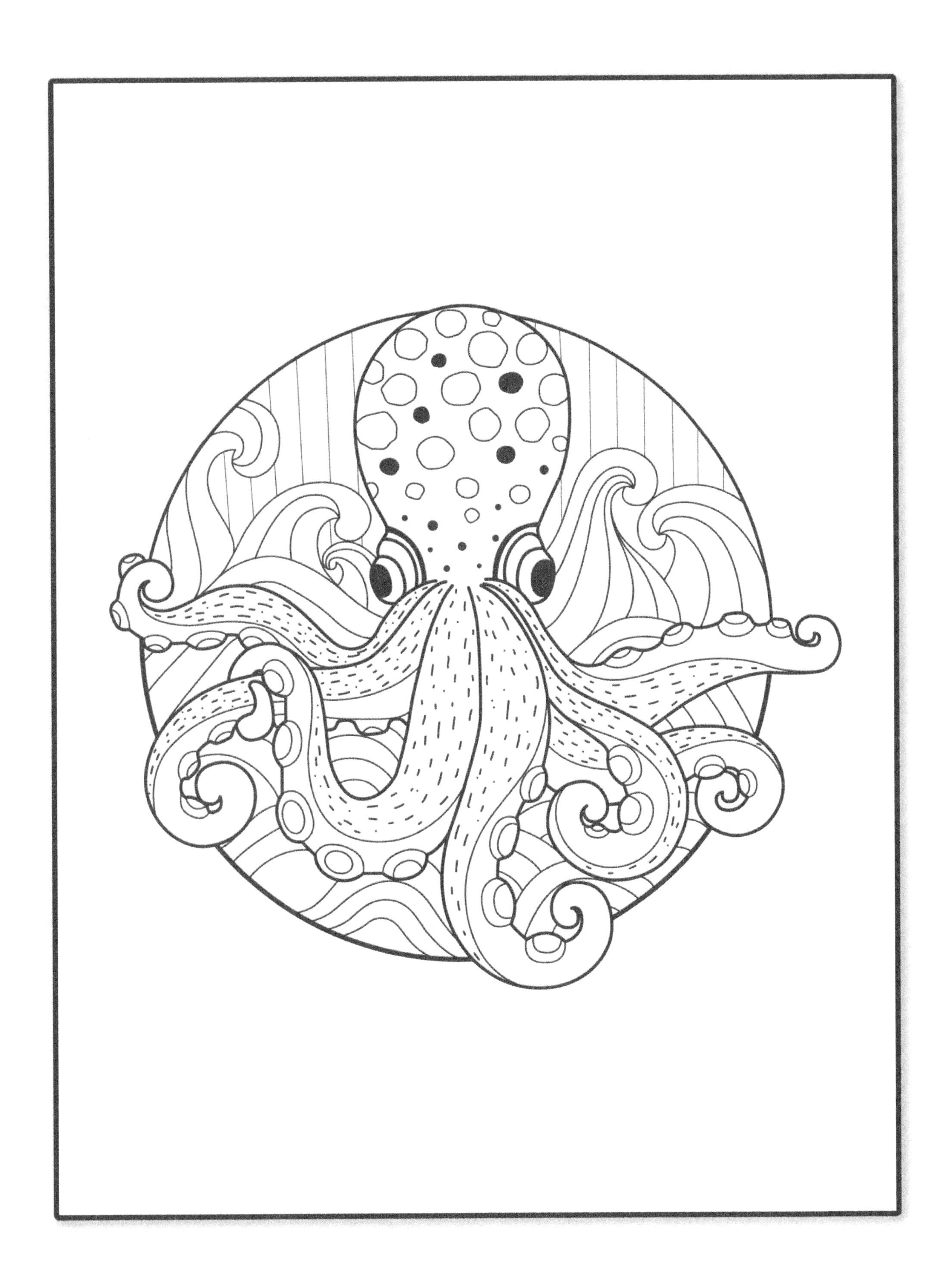

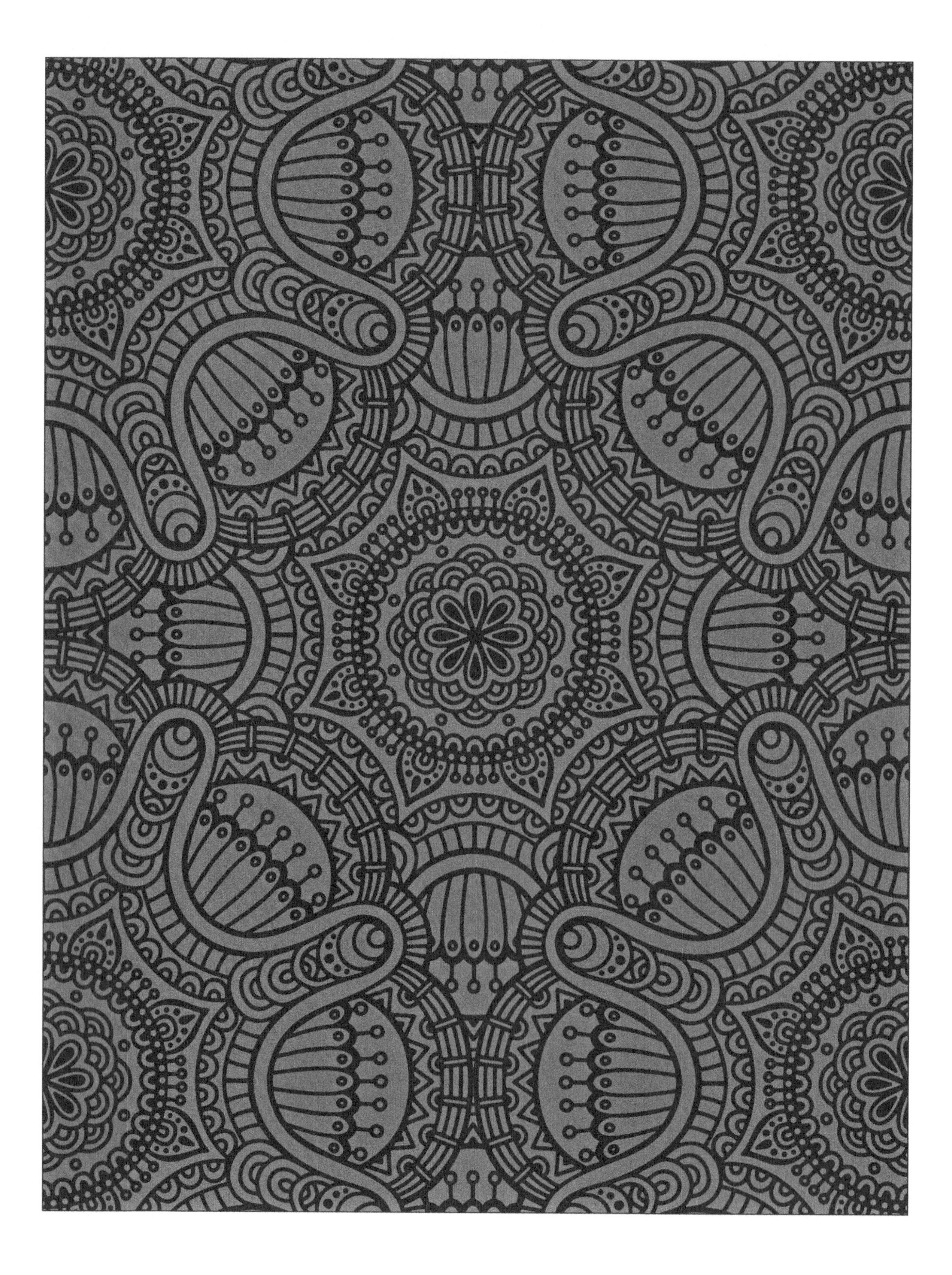

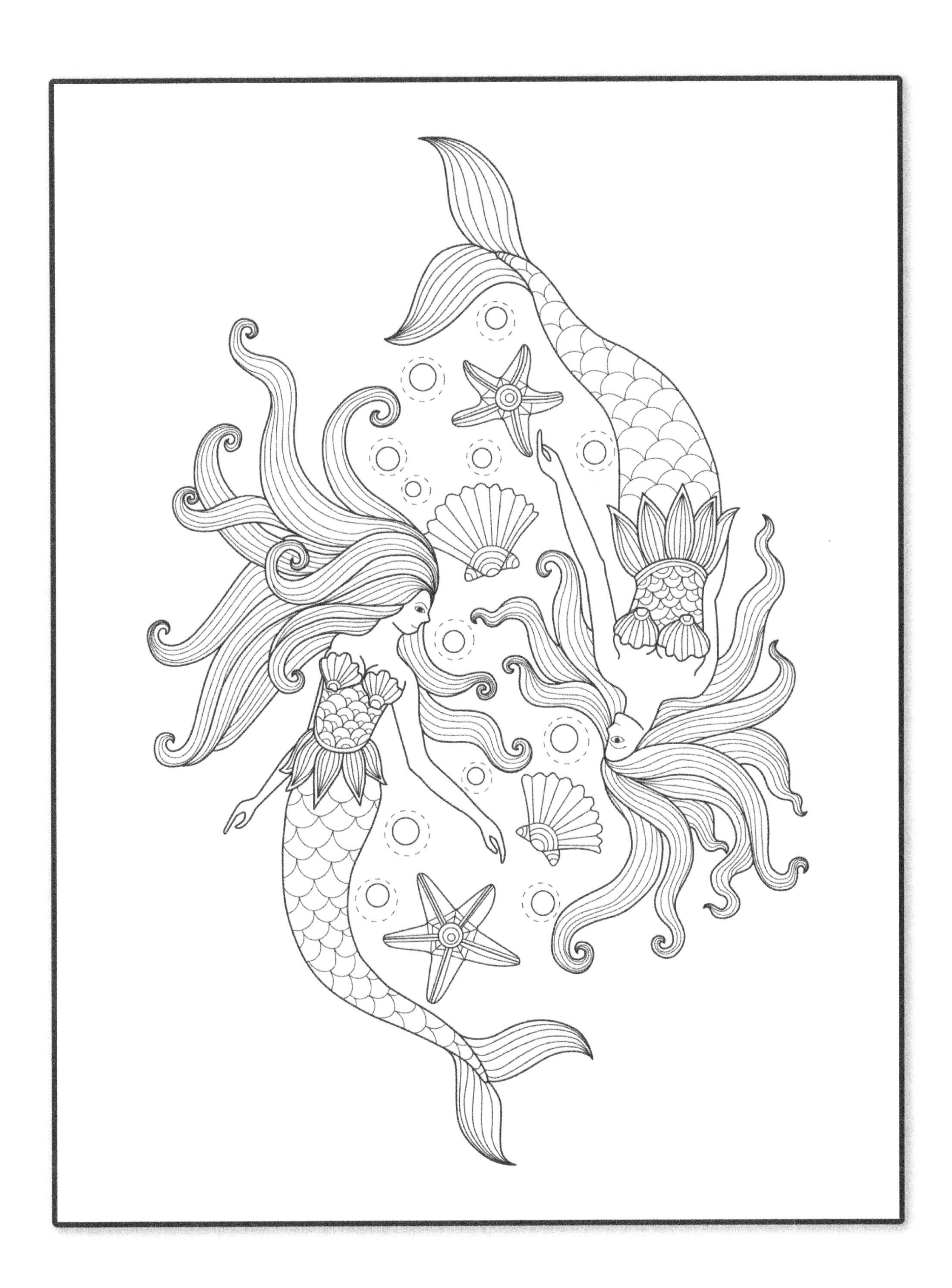

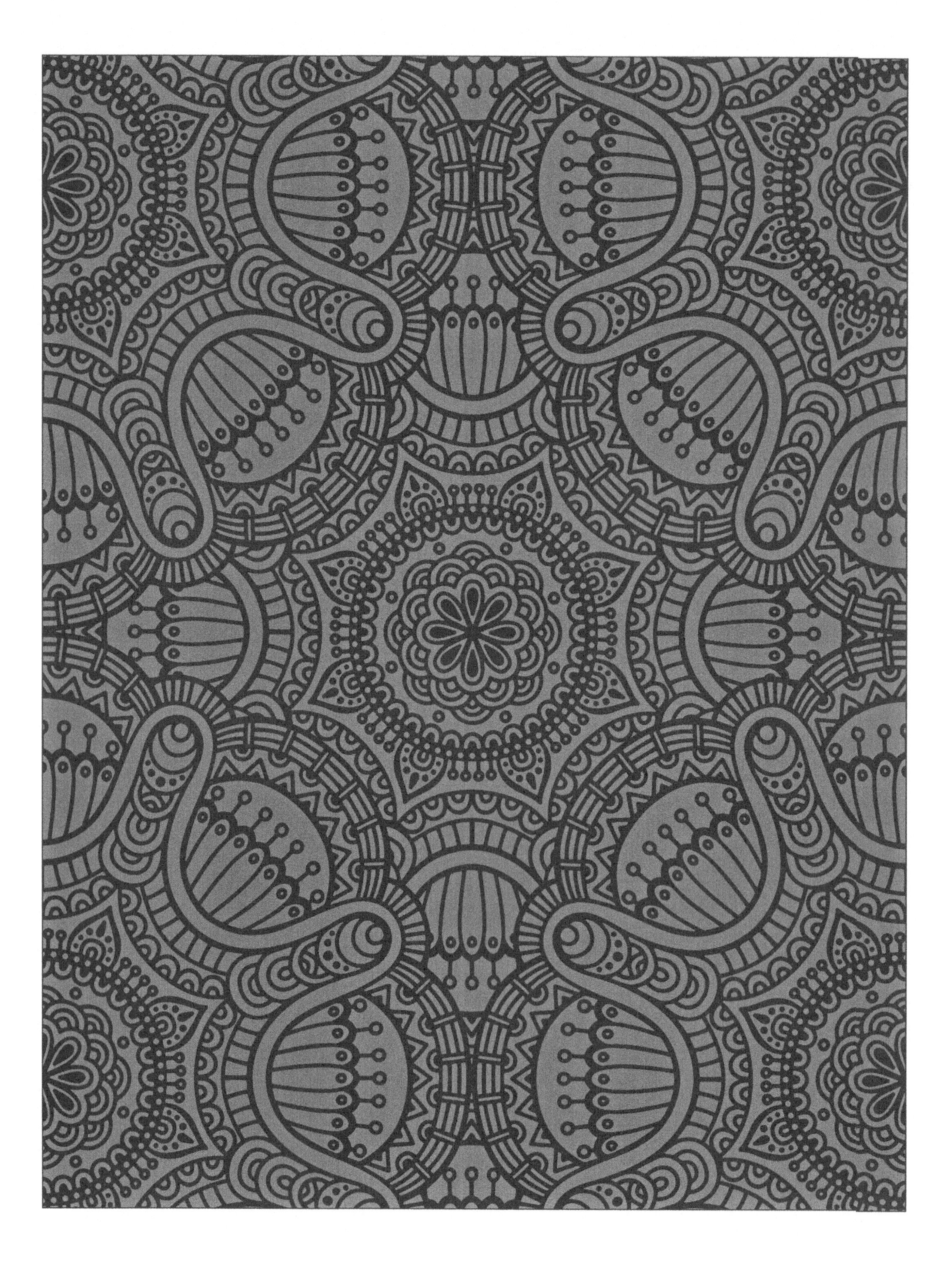

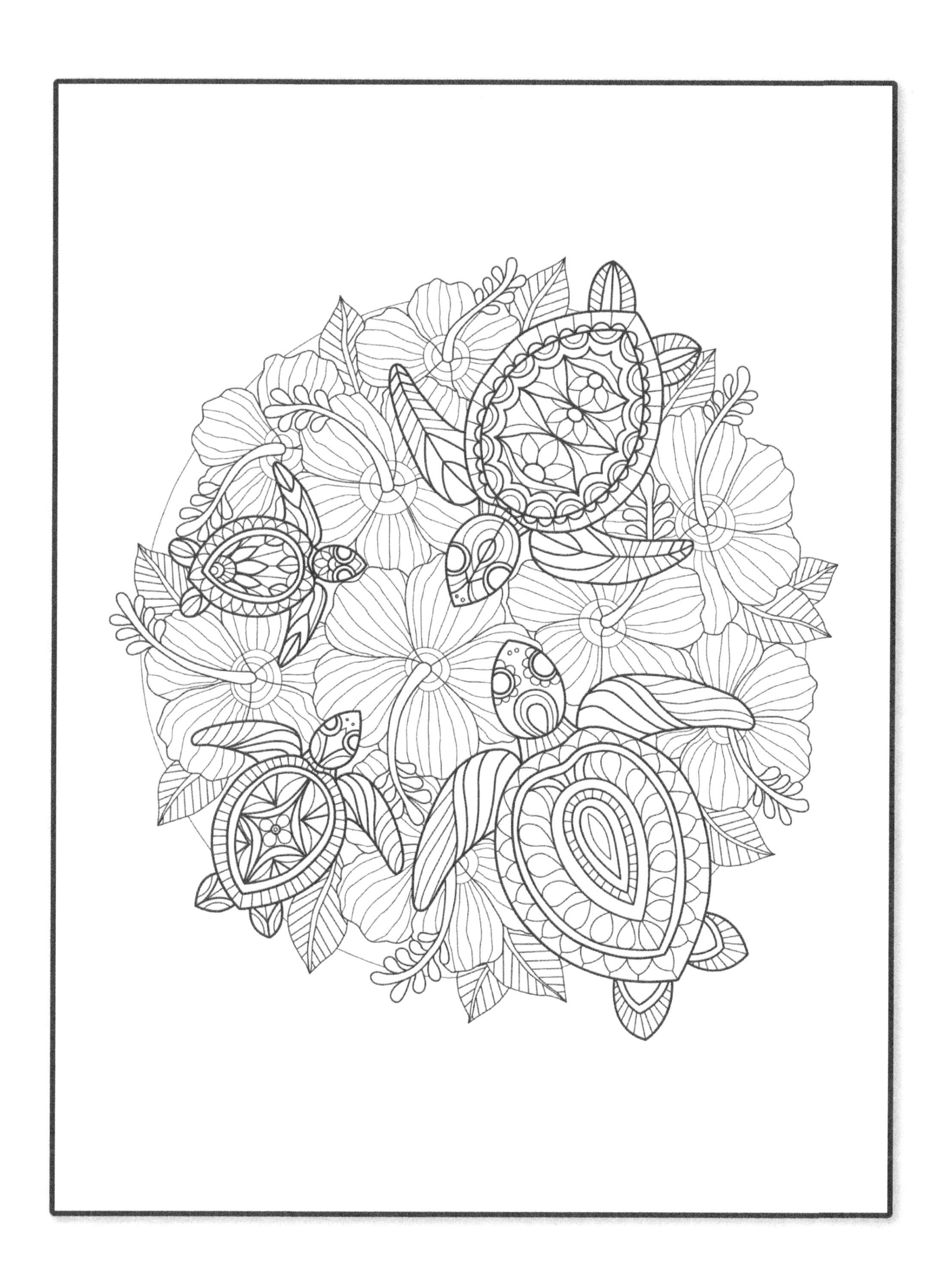

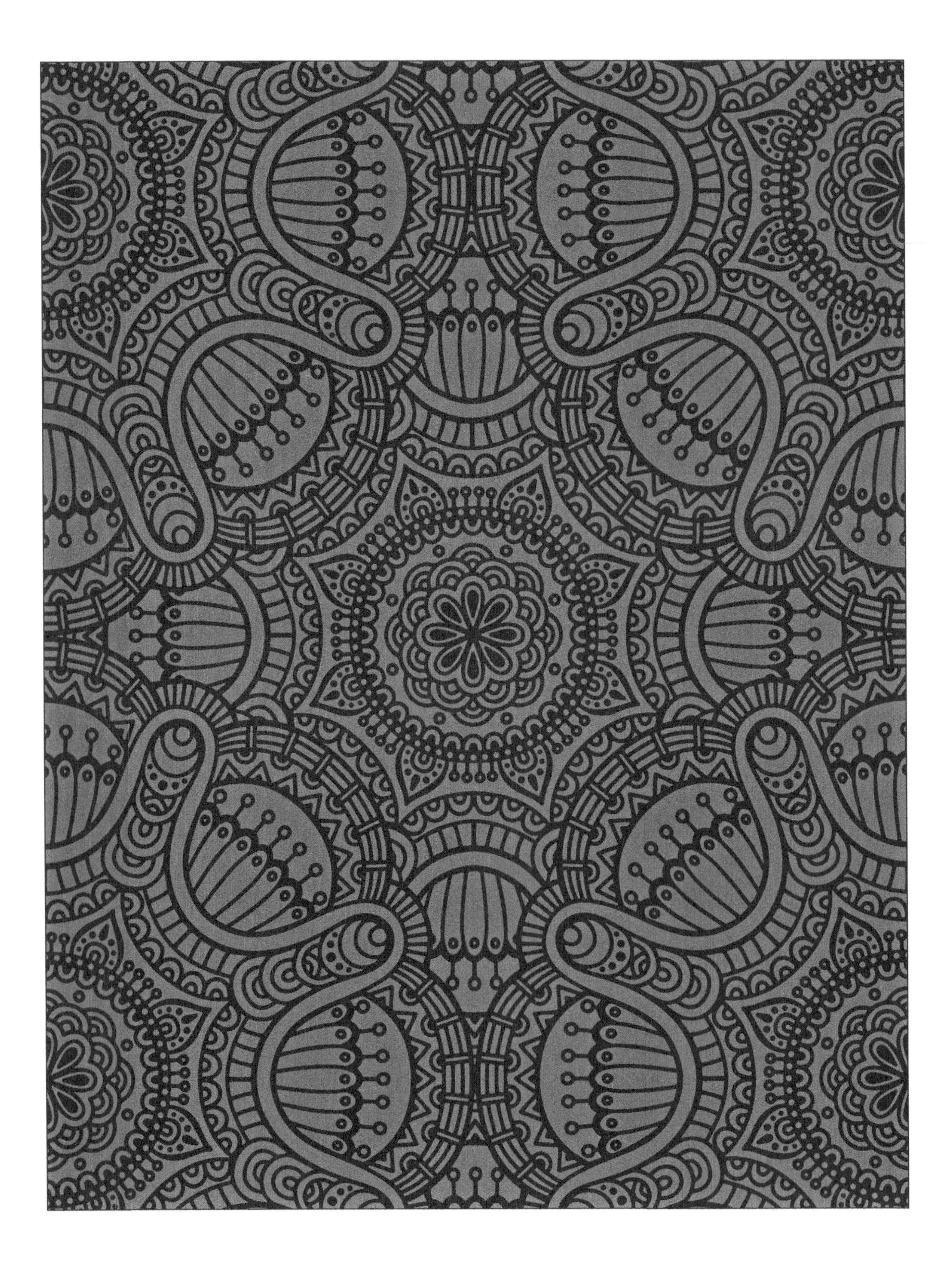

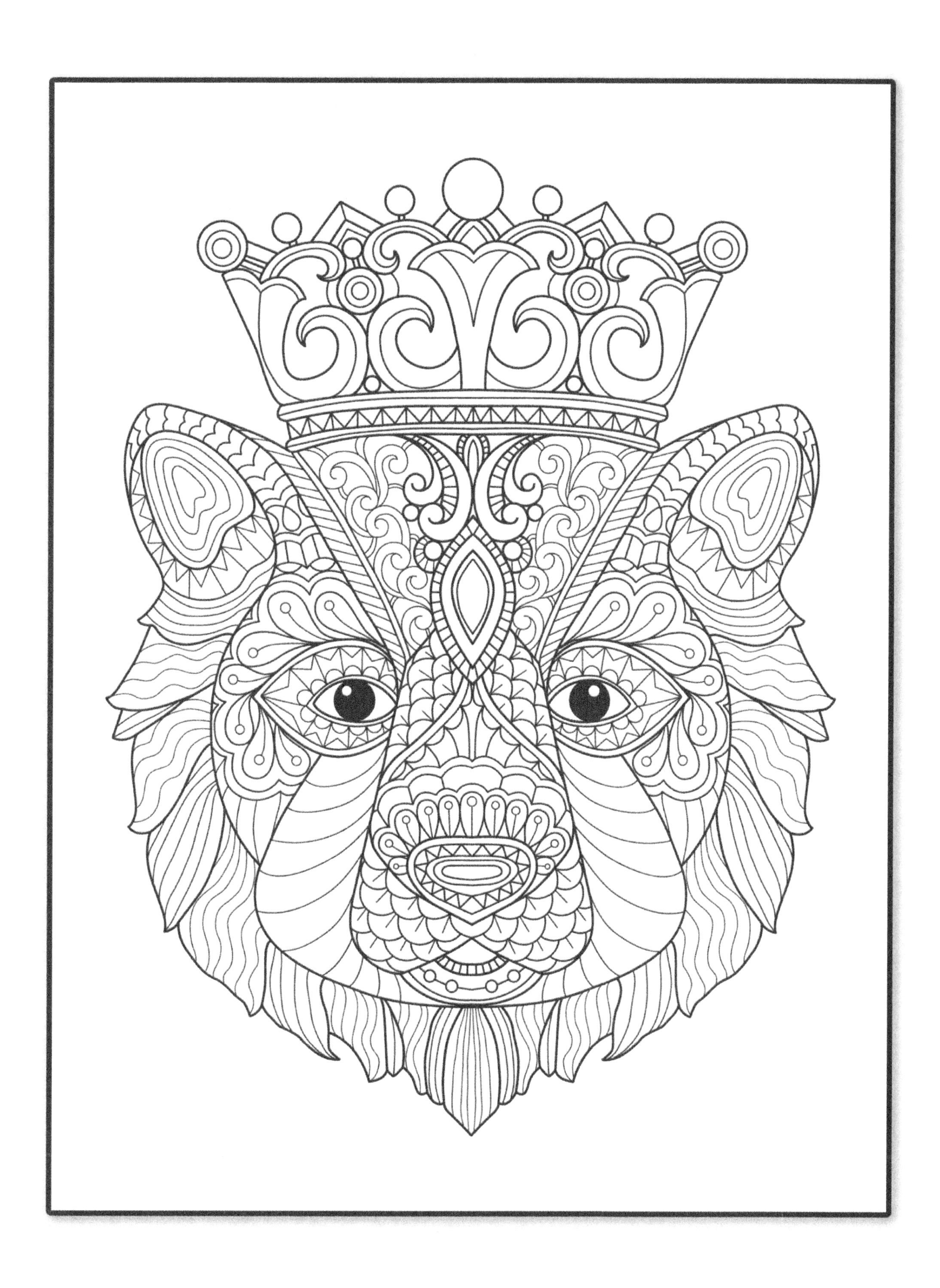

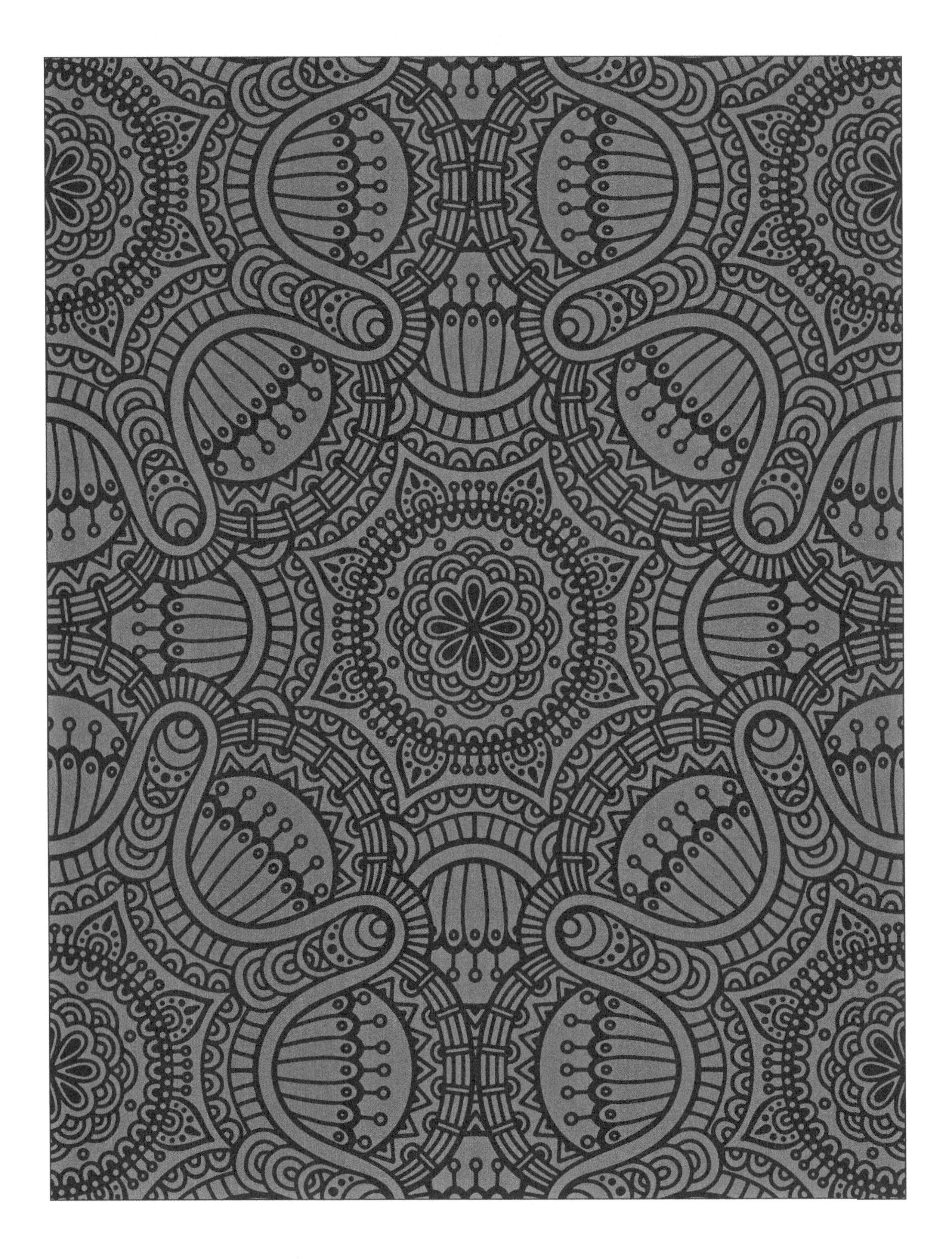

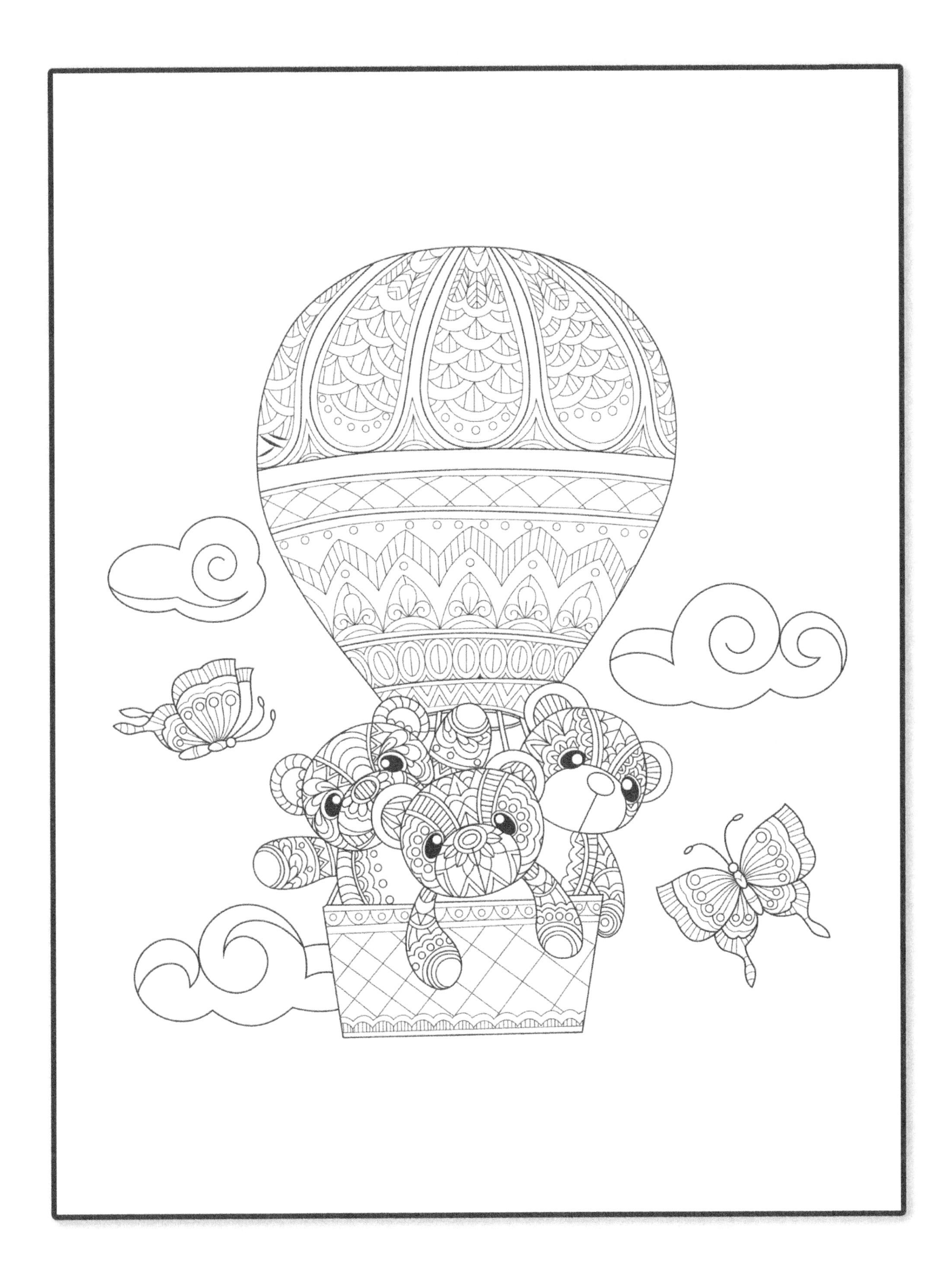

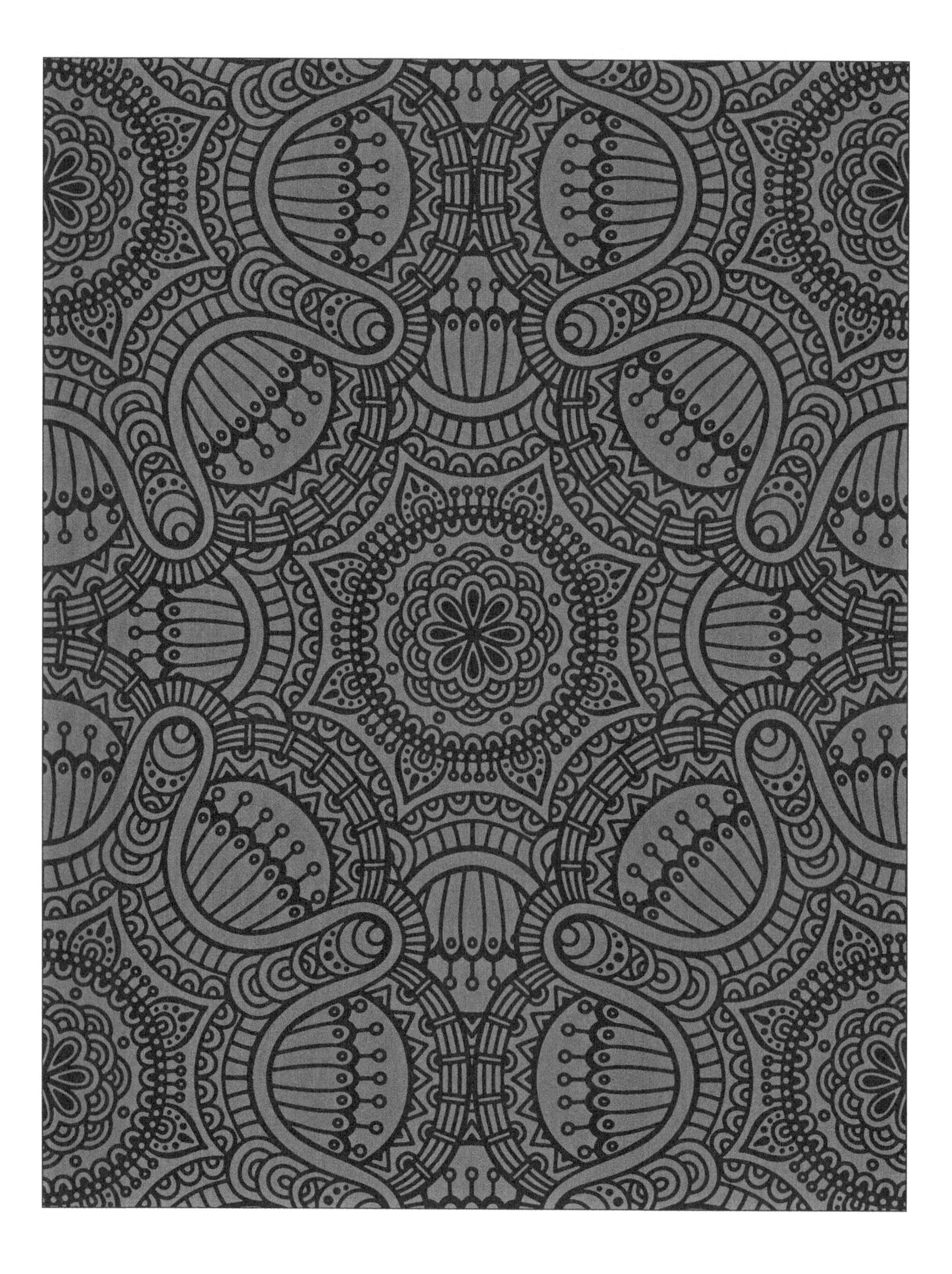

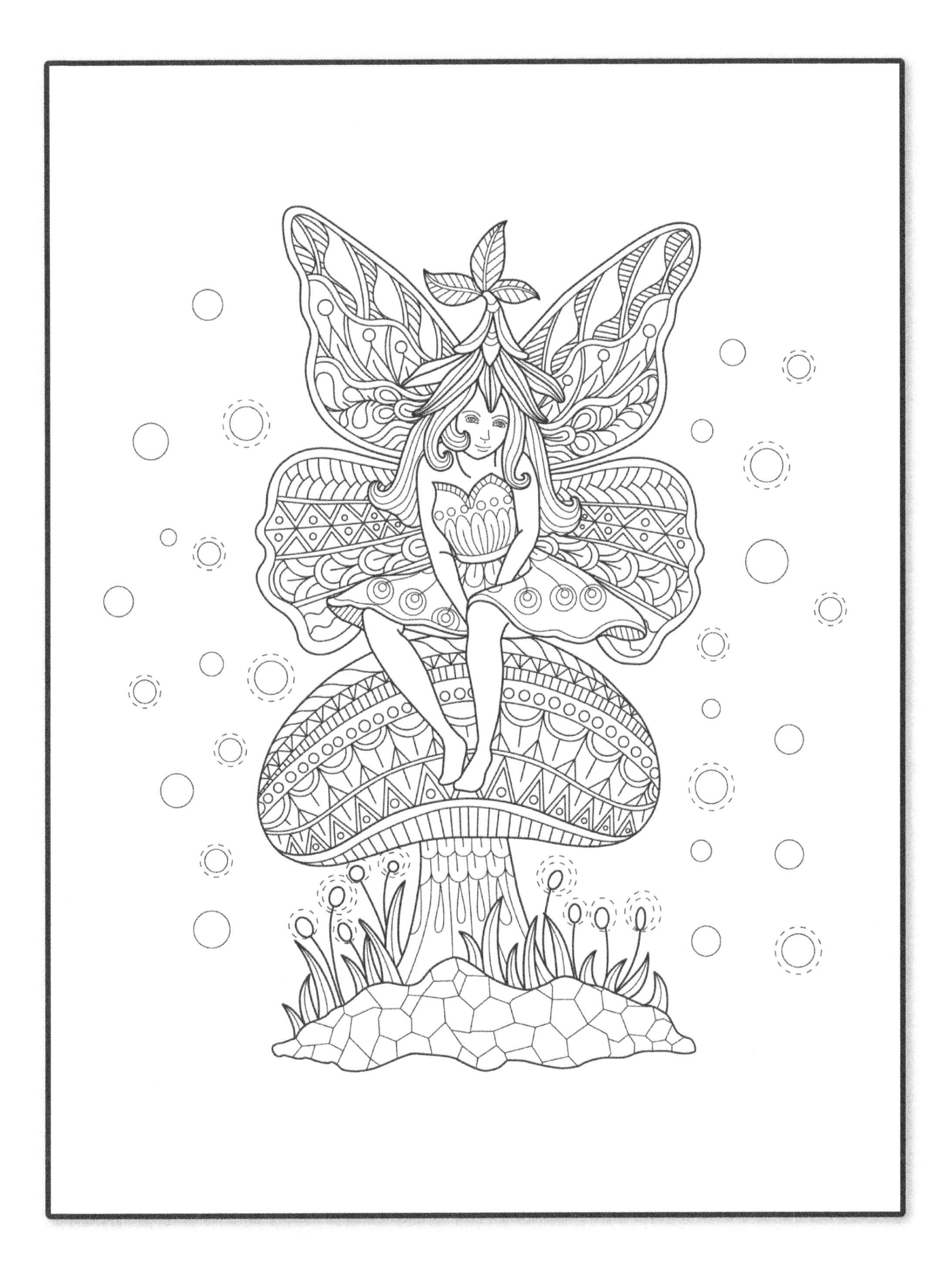

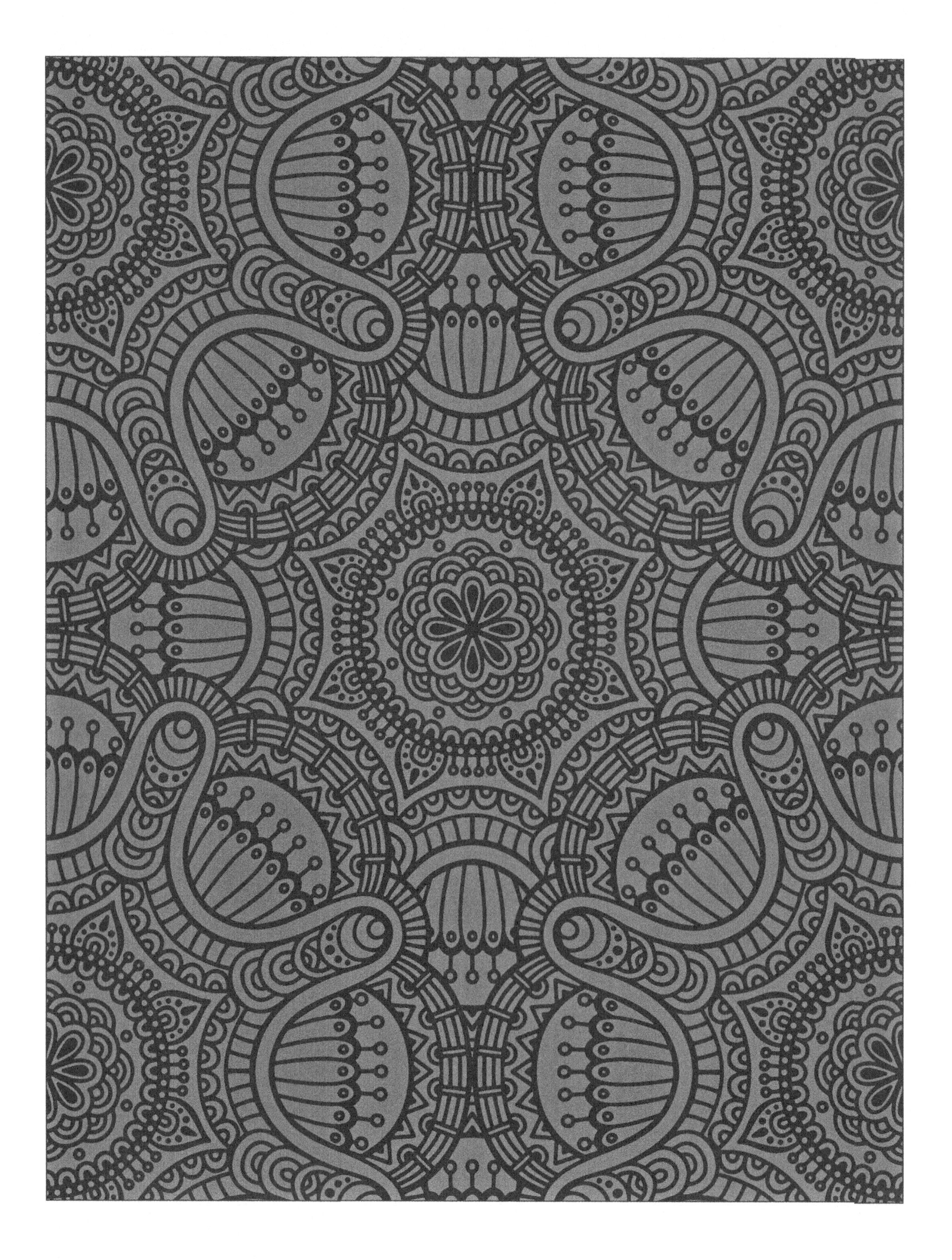

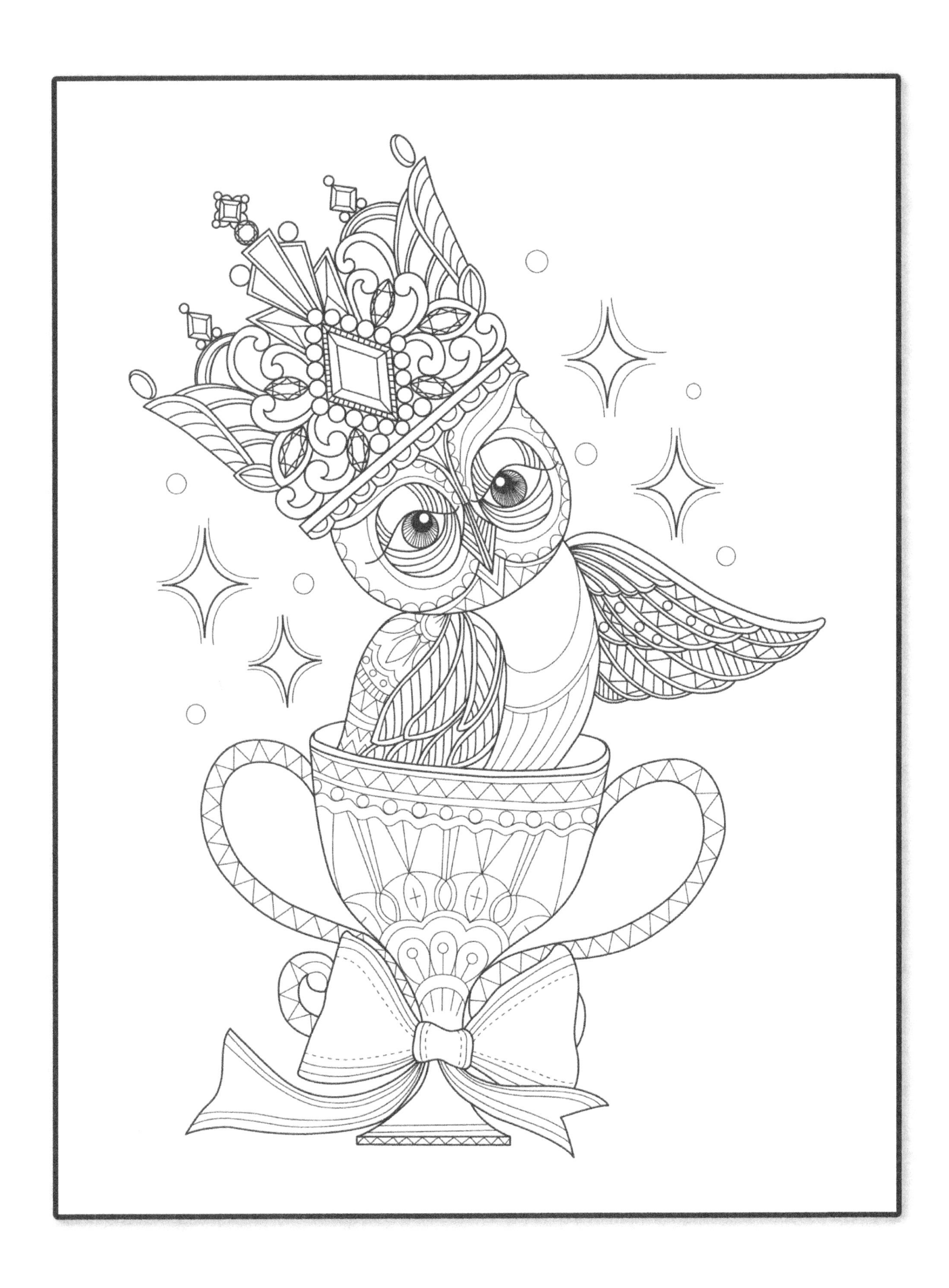

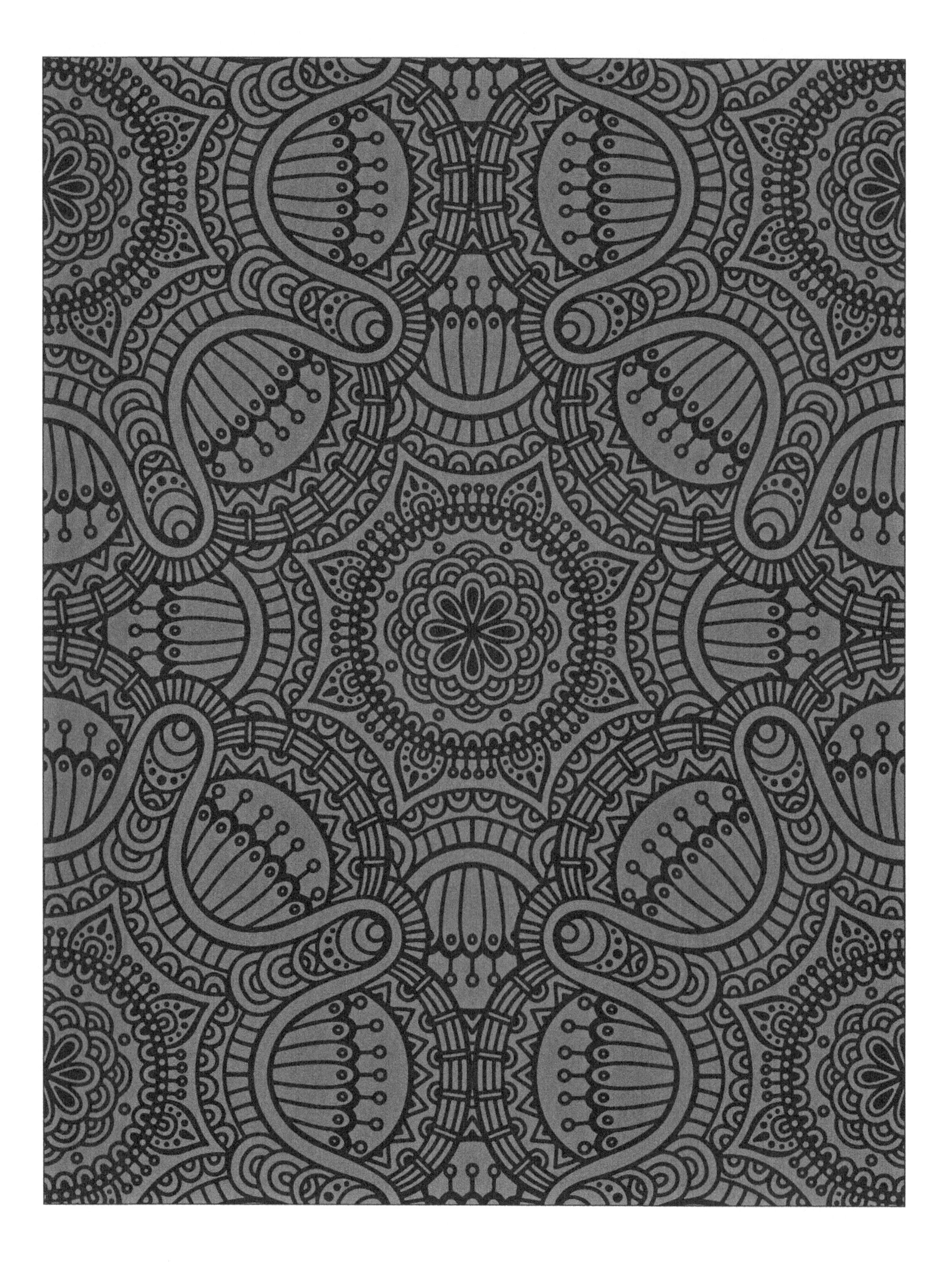

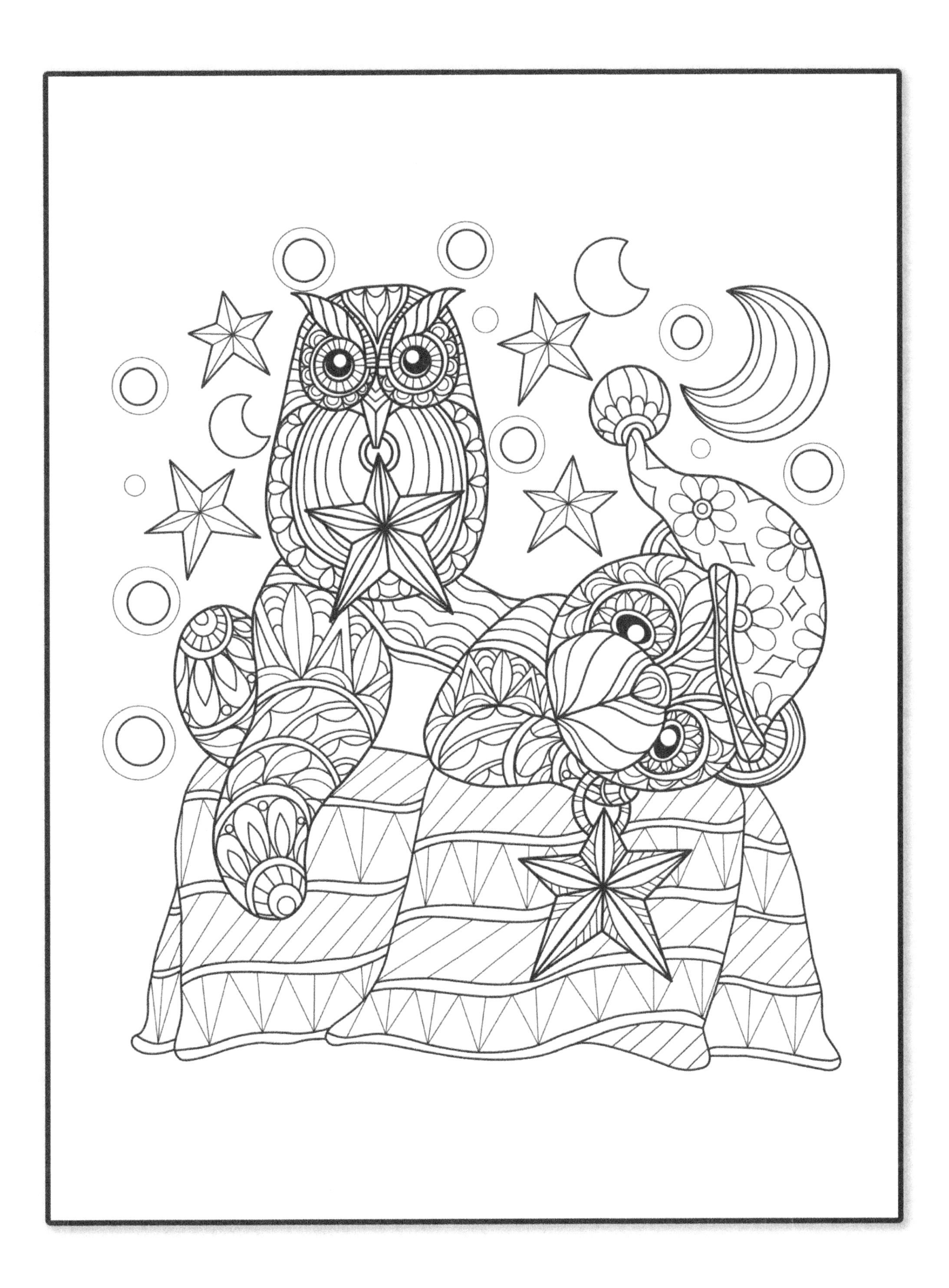

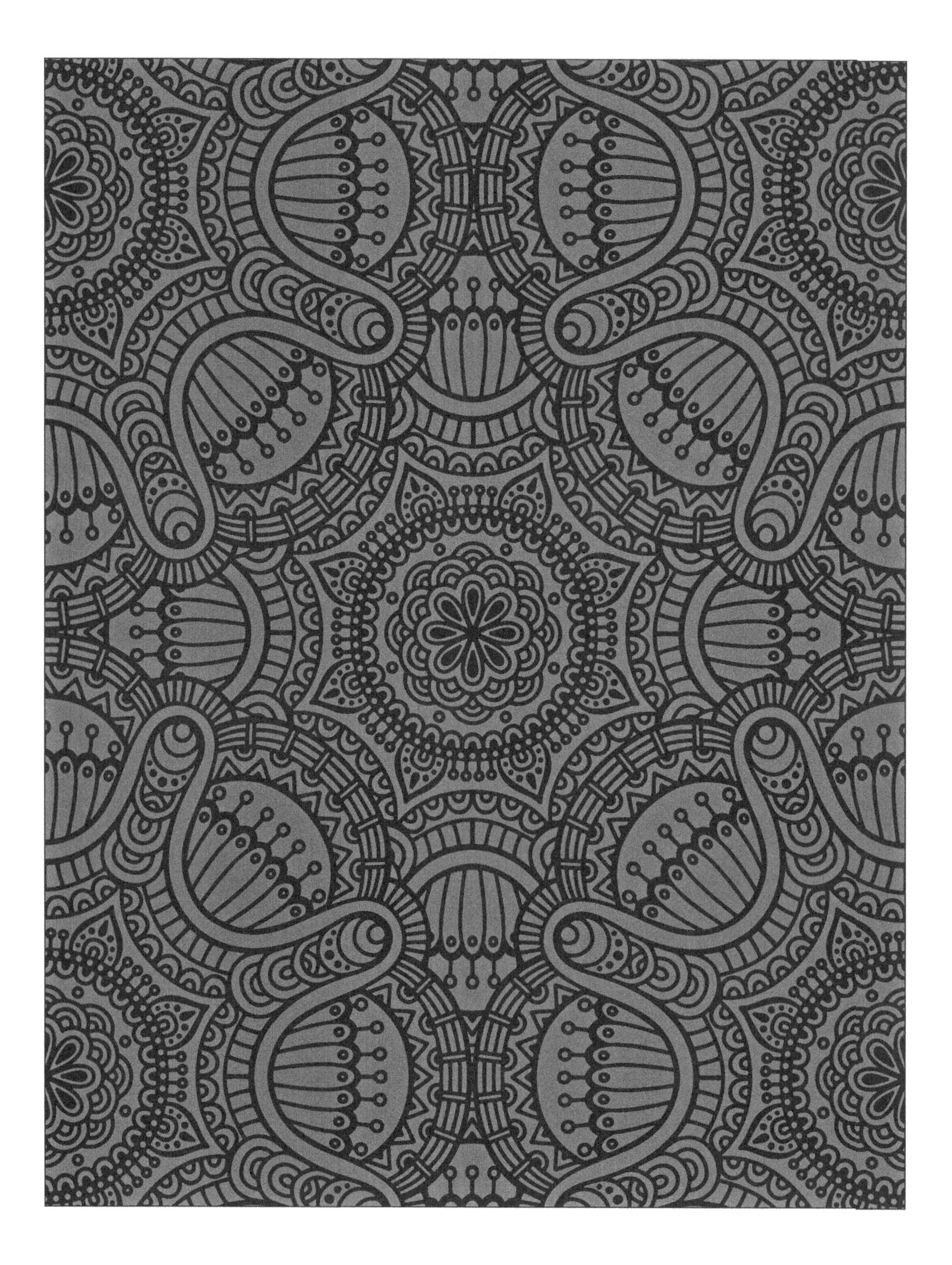

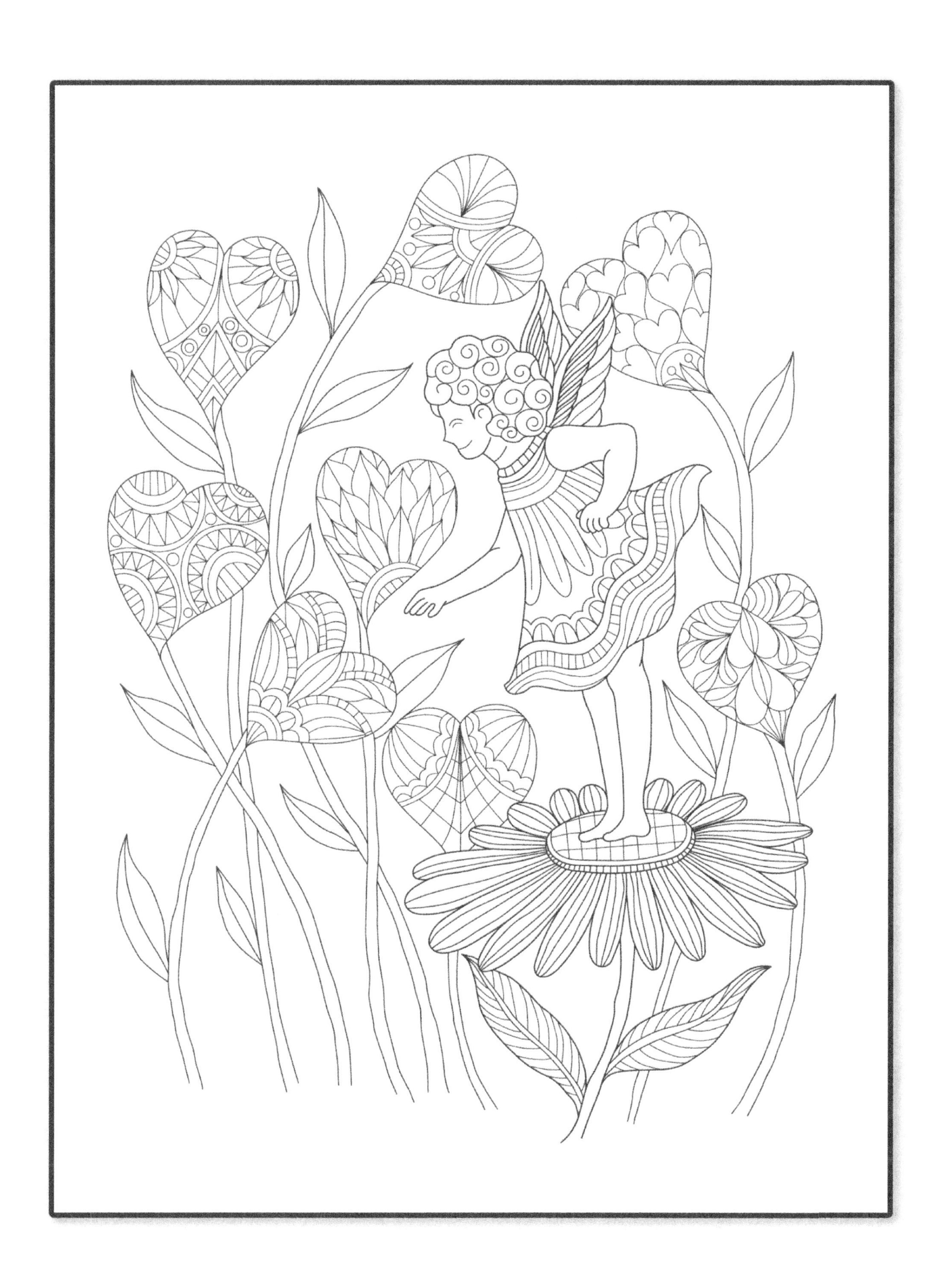

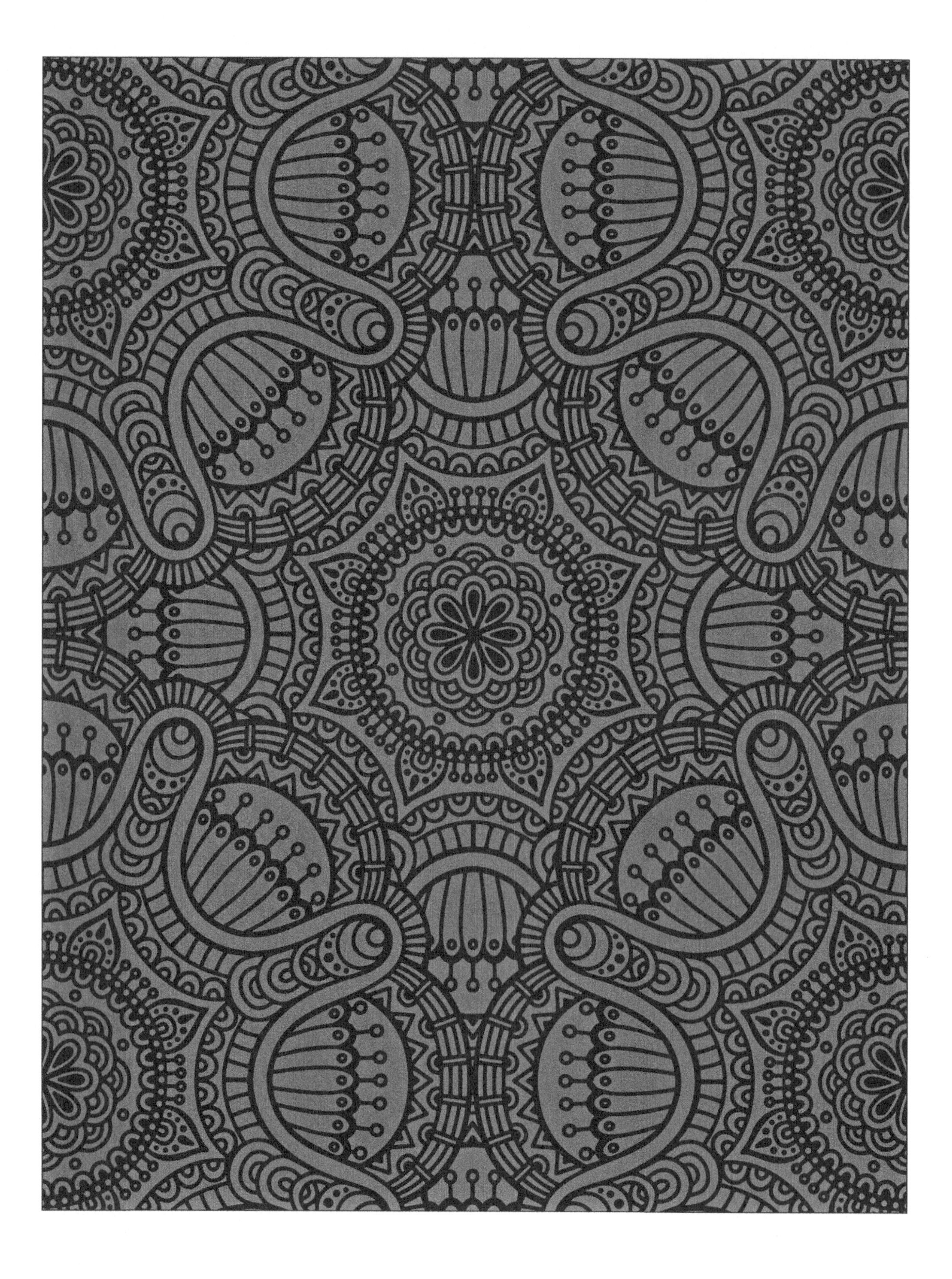

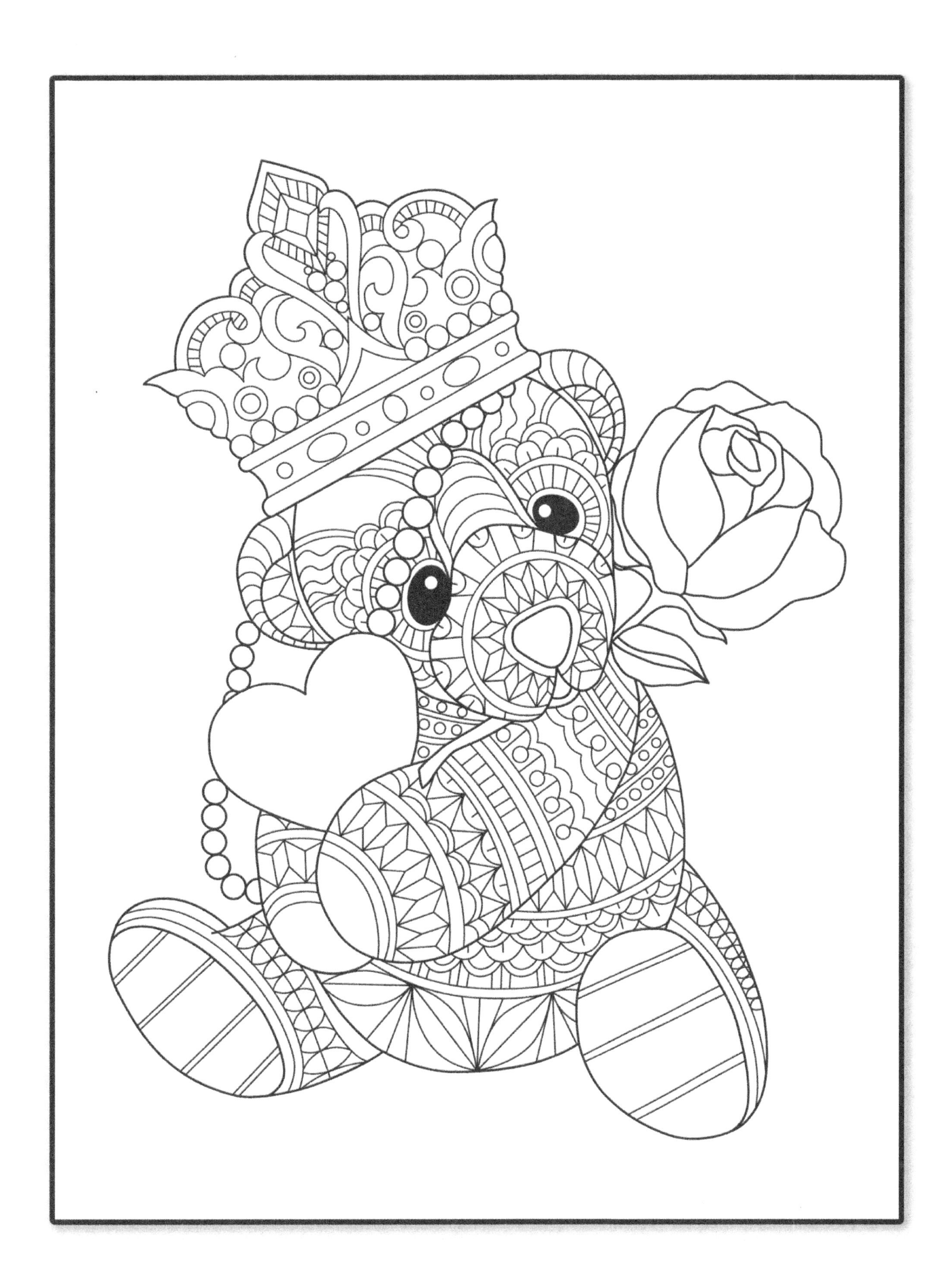

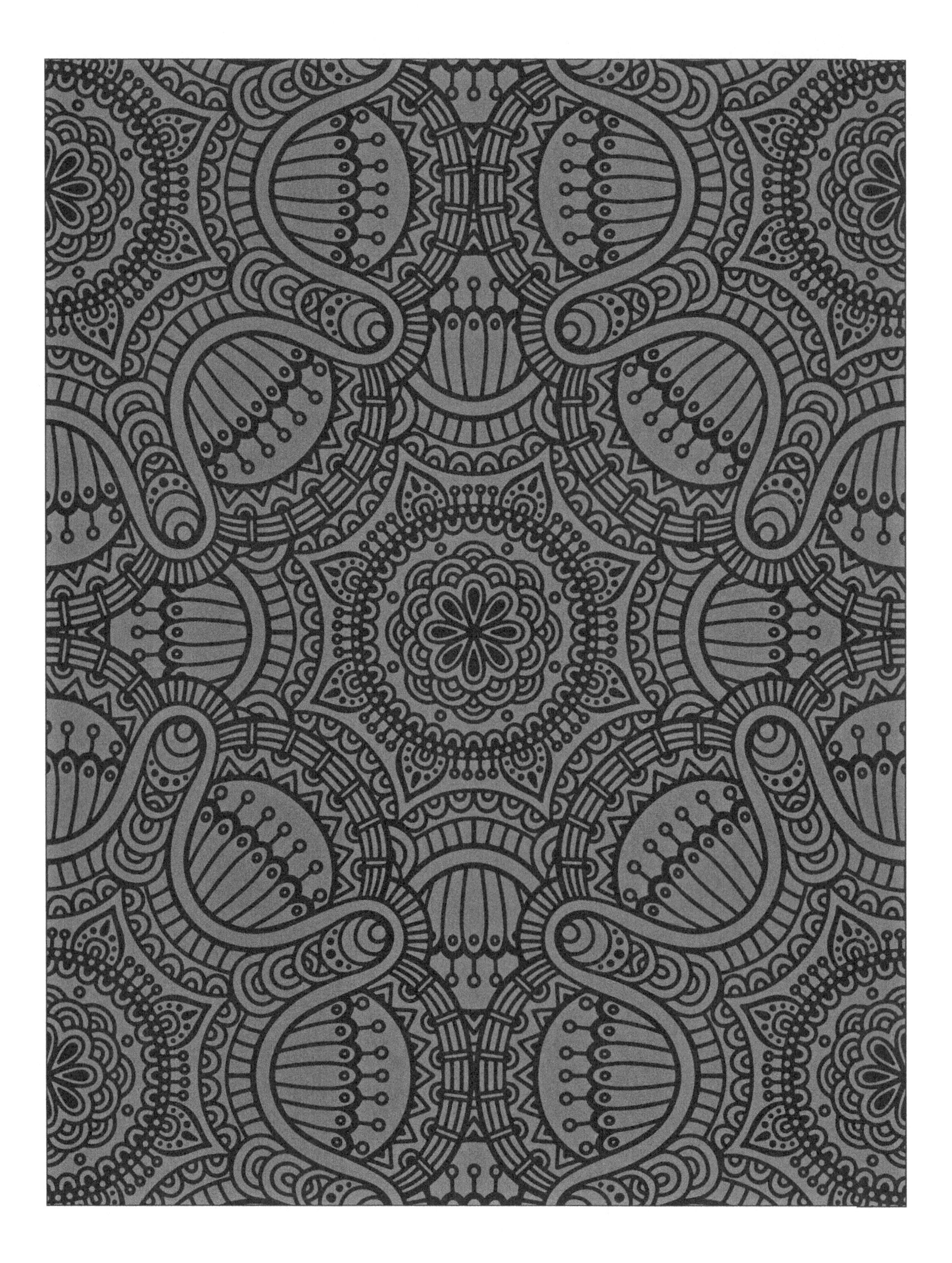

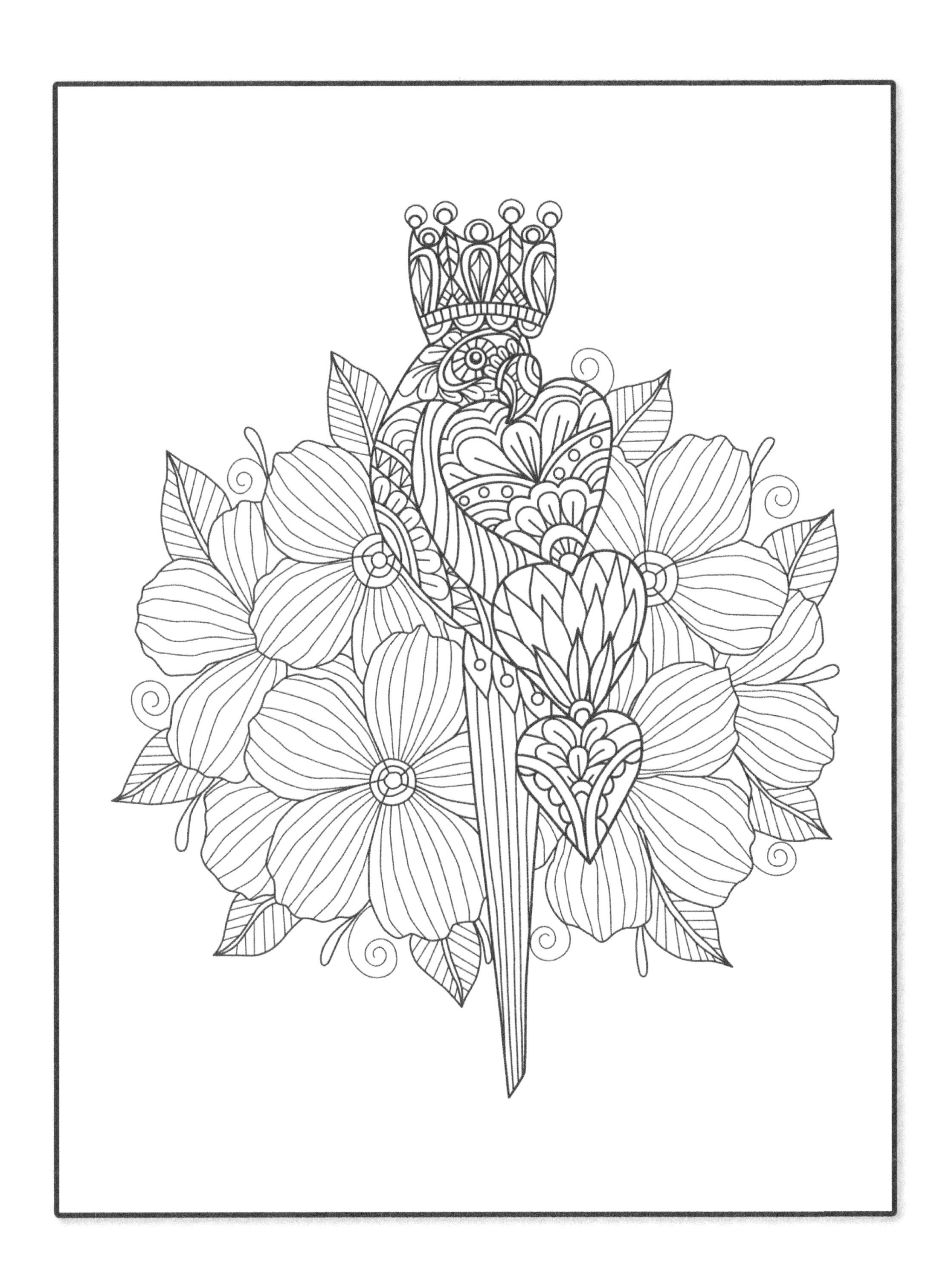

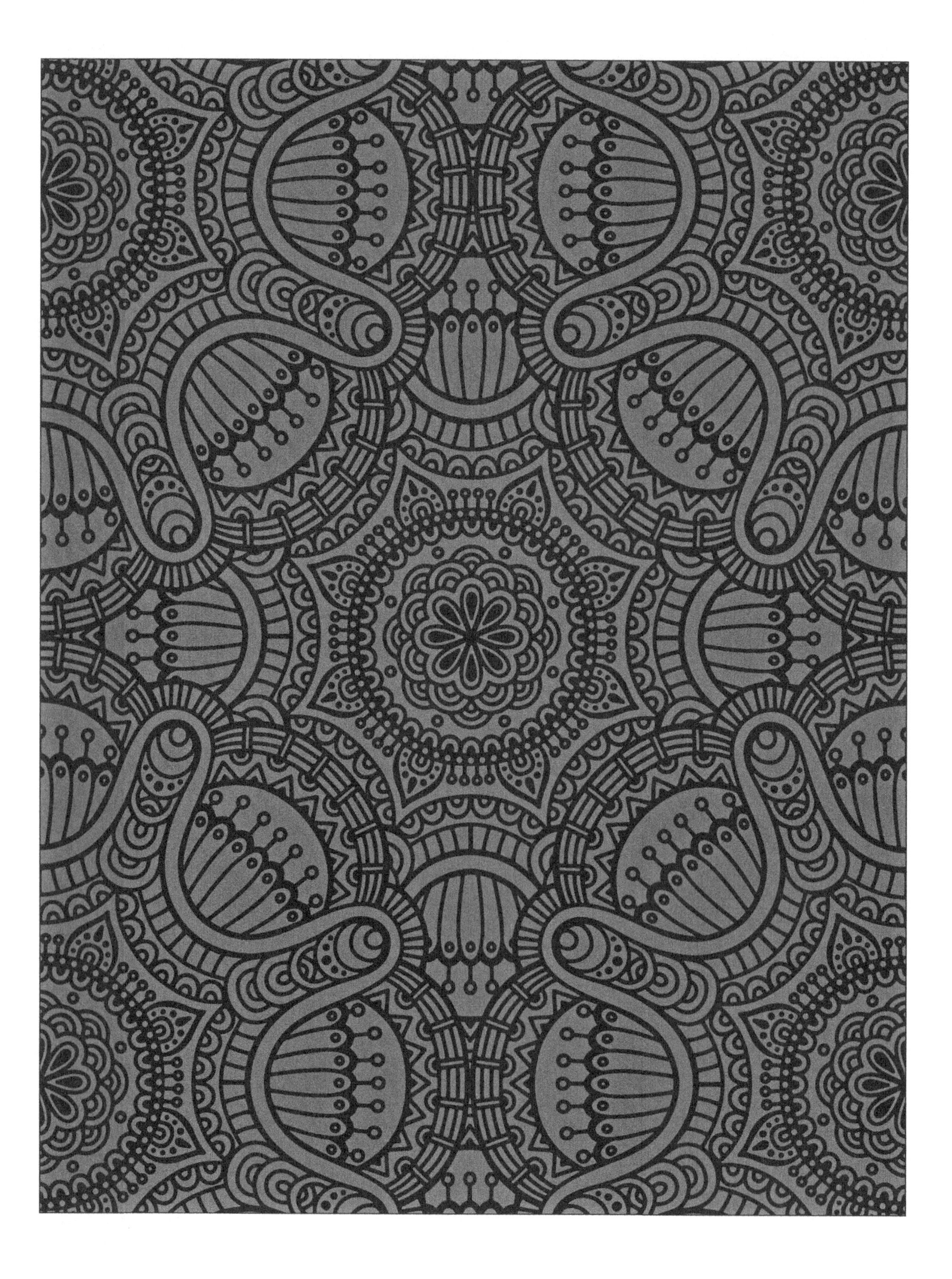

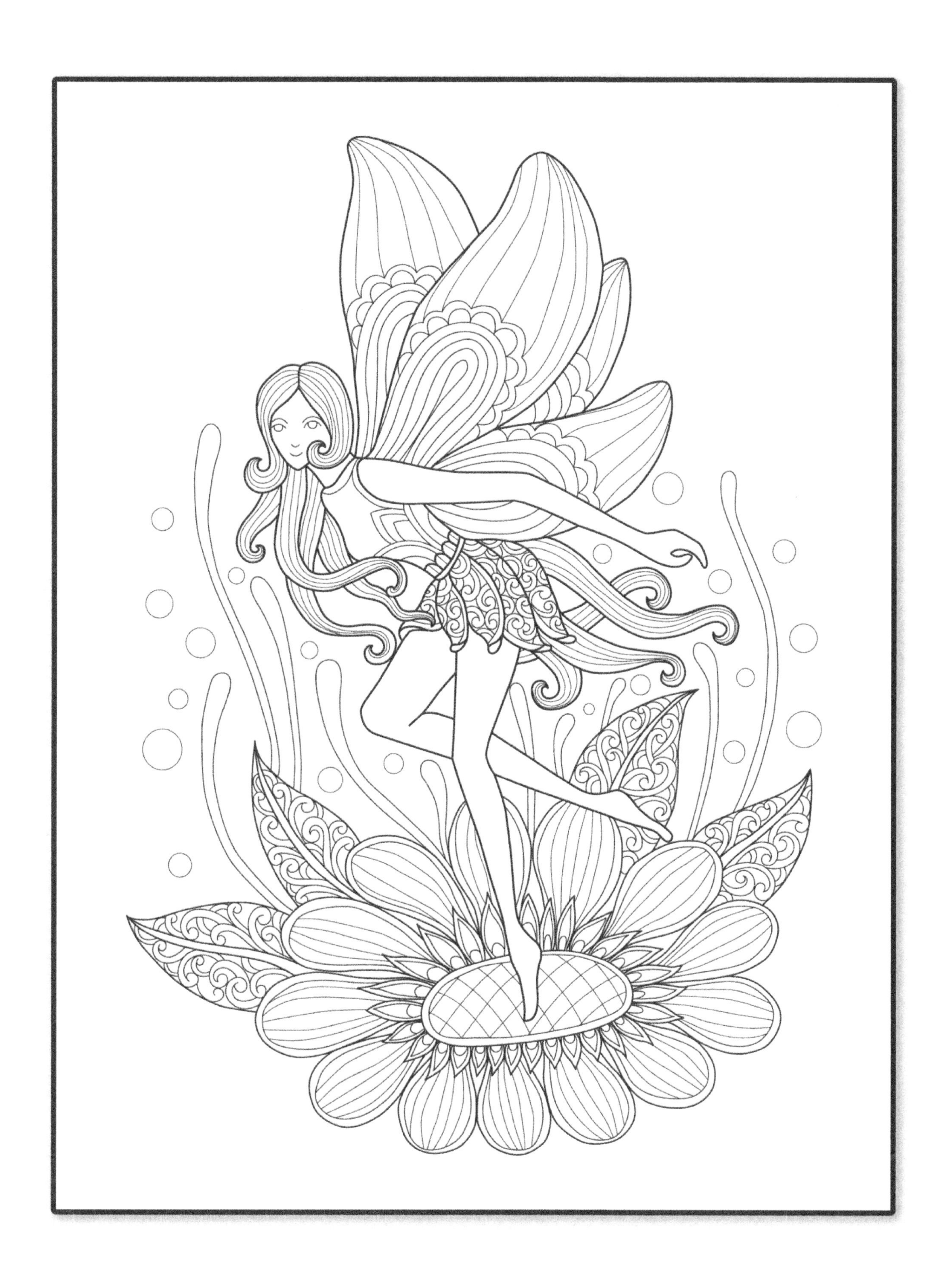

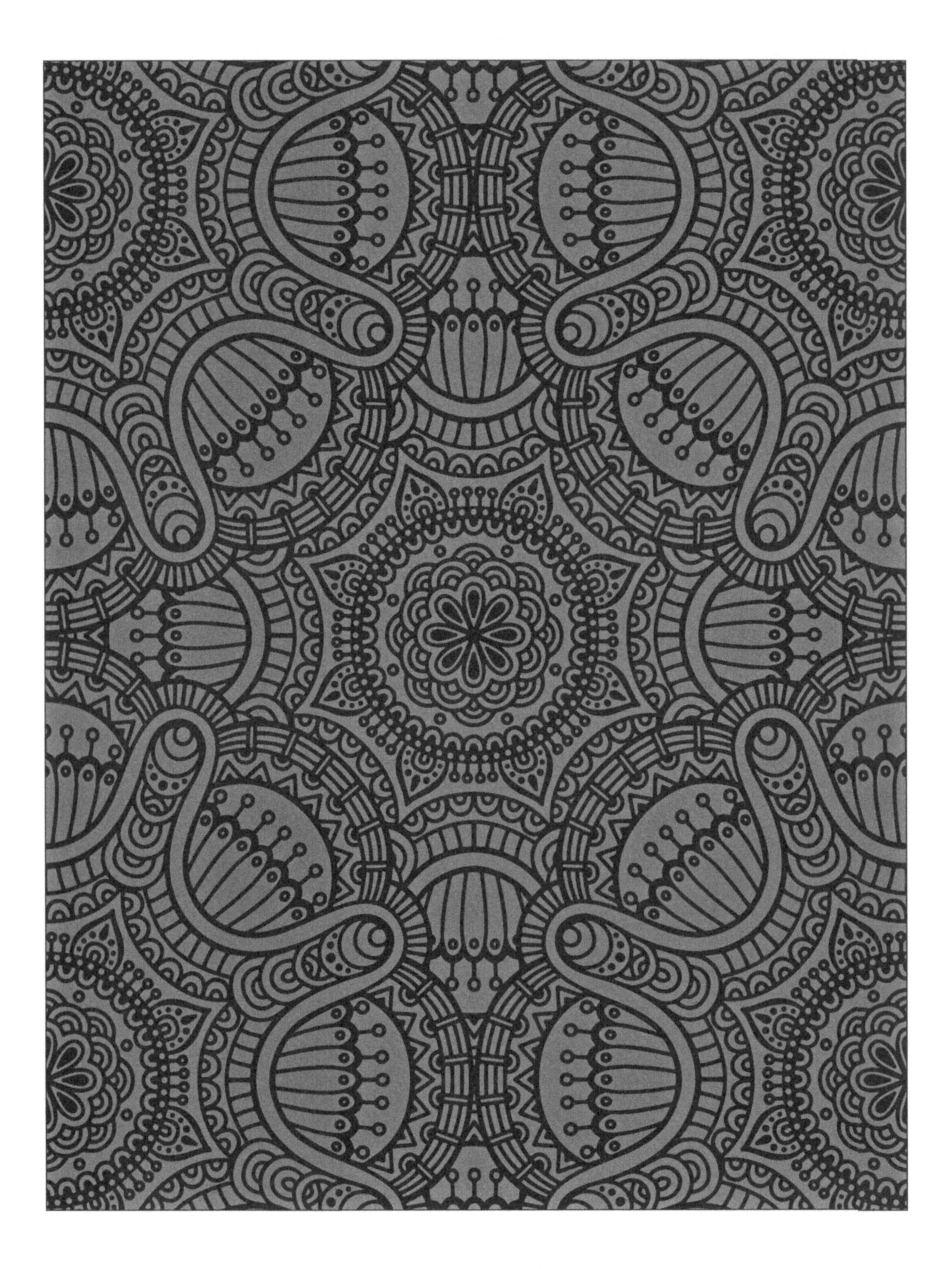

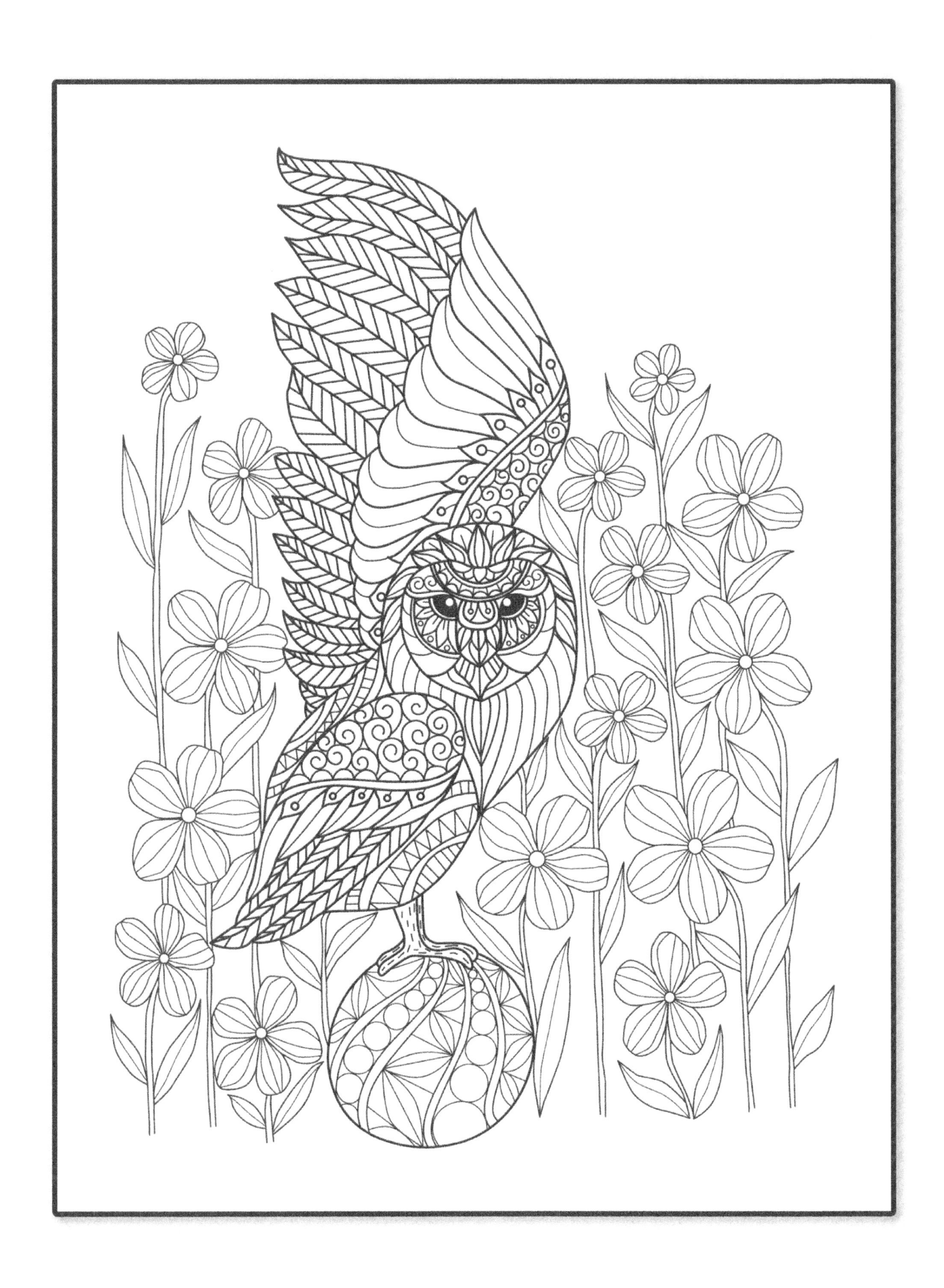

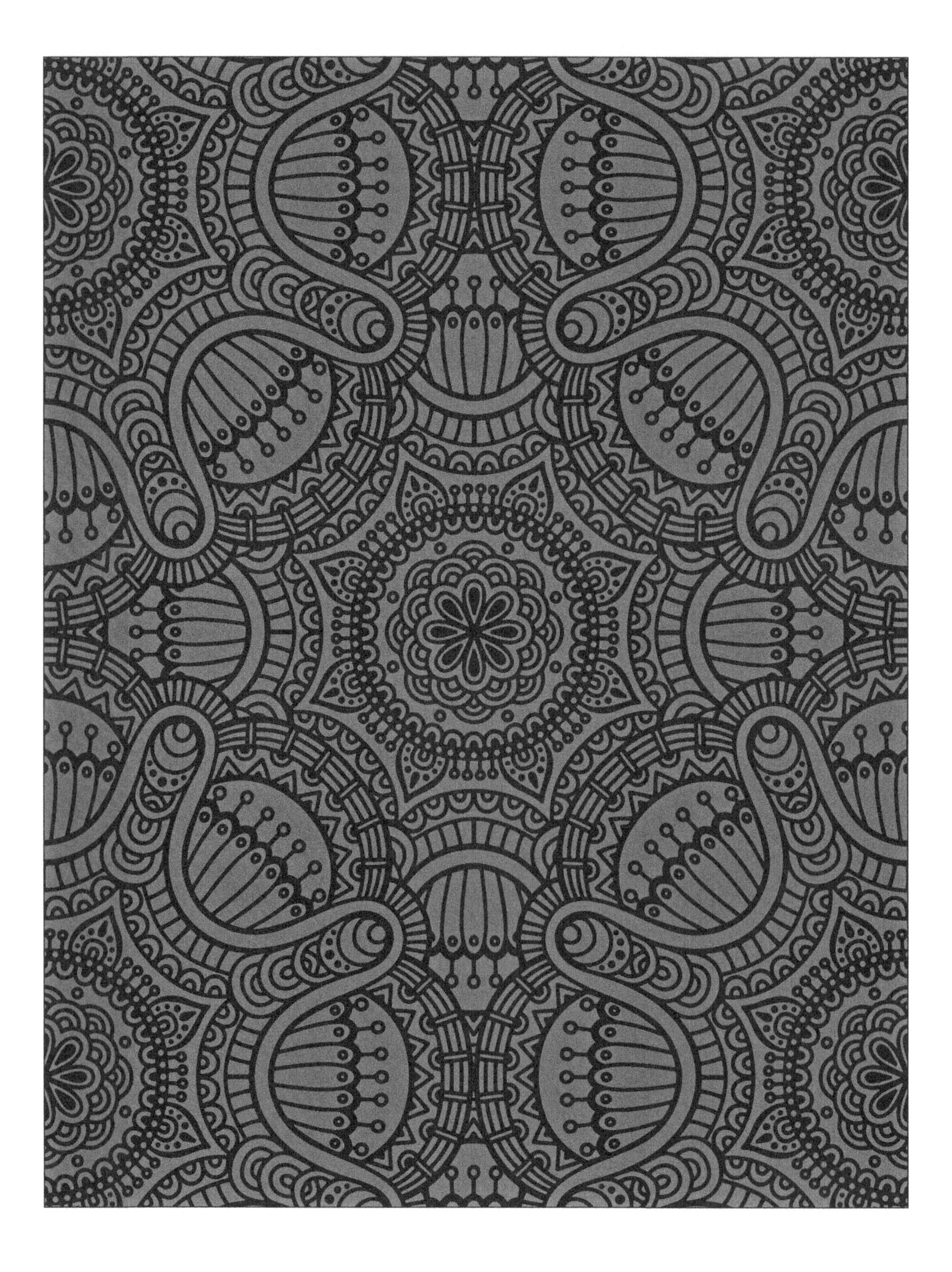

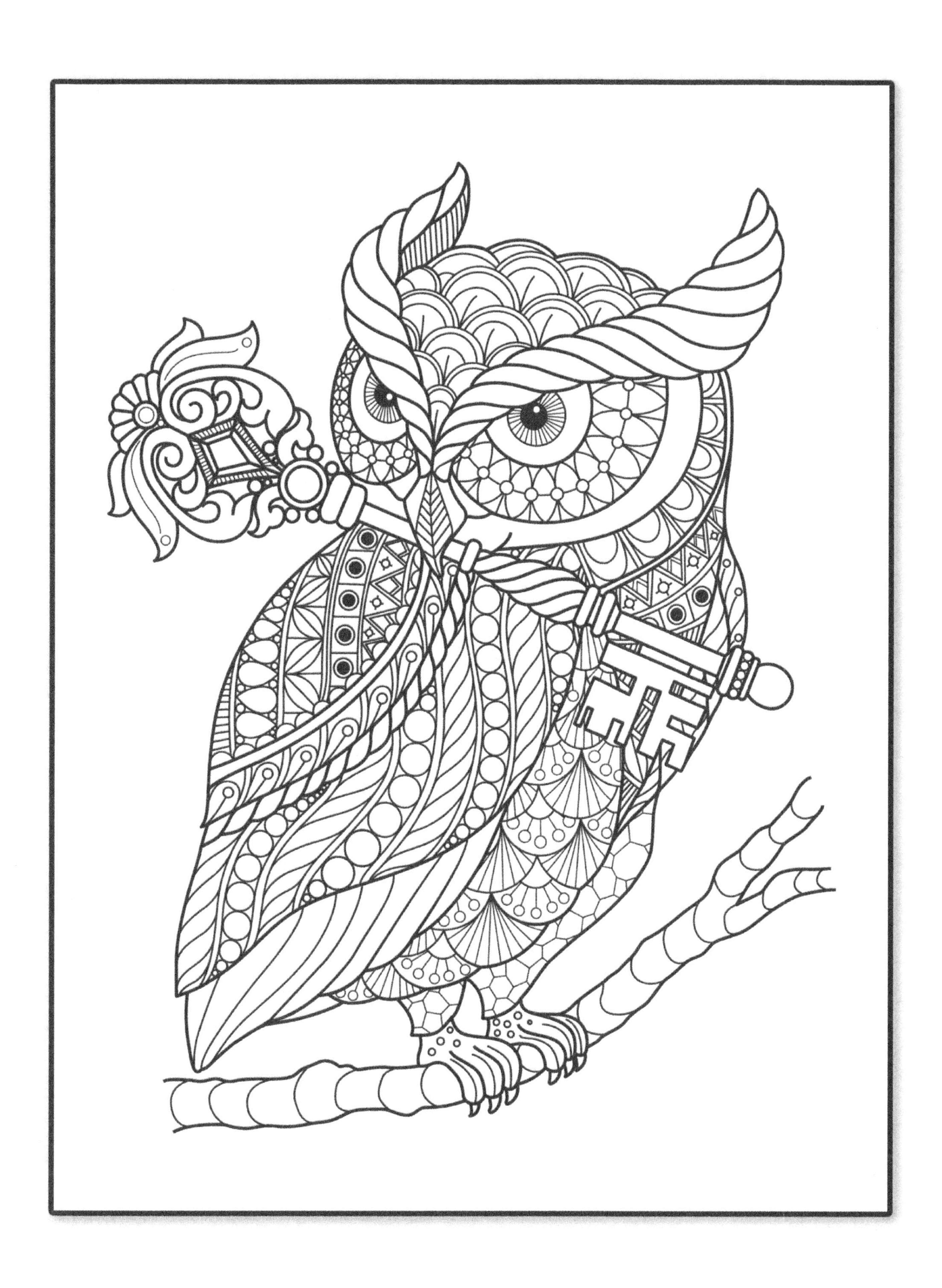

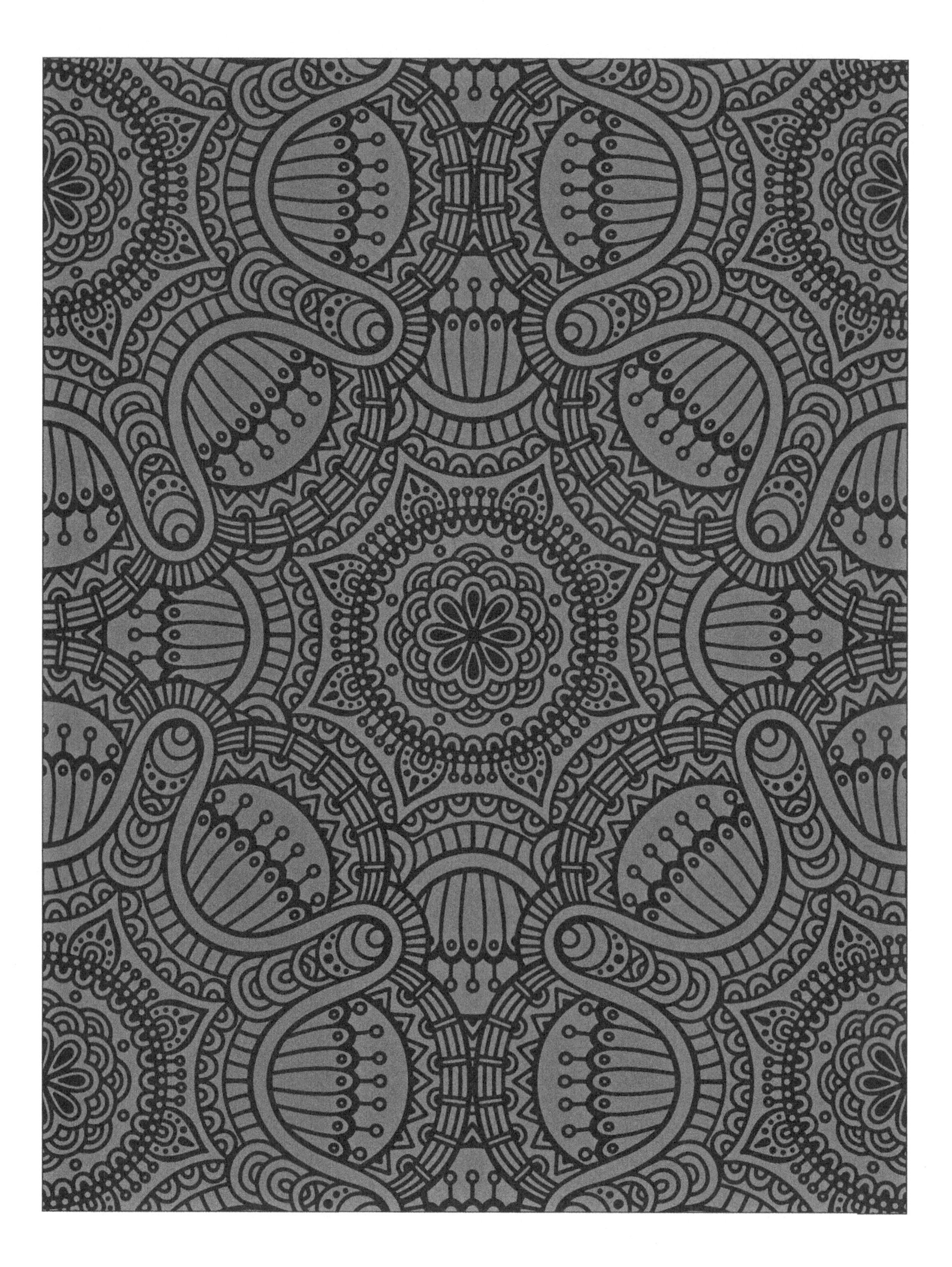

Color Test Page

Color Test Page

Made in the USA
Monee, IL
22 September 2022